School Reports to Parents

A study of policy and practice
in the secondary school

Brian Goacher
and
Margaret I. Reid

NFER–NELSON

Published by The NFER-NELSON Publishing Company Ltd.,
Darville House, 2 Oxford Road East,
Windsor, Berkshire SL4 1DF

First Published 1983
© National Foundation for Educational Research, 1983
ISBN 0–7005–0611 X
Code 8094 021

Typeset by Cambrian Typesetters, Aldershot,
Hants

Printed and bound in Great Britain
by Billing & Sons Limited, Worcester.

Project Staff (April 1978 to March 1981)

Principal Research Officer   Margaret I. Reid
Senior Research Officer (Project Leader)   Brian J. Goacher
Assistant Research Officer   Richard Weindling (1.4.78 to 30.9.79)
     Ursula de Kock (19.11.79 to 30.11.80)
Project Statistician   Peter Smedley
Project Secretary   Mrs Ann Symmonds

Contents

Acknowledgements

Our thanks go first to the heads, teachers, parents and students who took part in this study and who gave so much of their time to answering our questions about the reports they compiled or received. An inquiry of the kind reported in this book would not have been possible without their unstinting help.

We are grateful, too, to colleagues both in the Foundation and outside who assisted in various parts of the study. In particular, we would like to thank Miss Ursula de Kock who, as assistant research officer, shared in the fieldwork in schools and in the coding and ordering of the data. Richard Weindling assisted in developing the questionnaires in the early stages of the project and again at the end with editing the report, whilst Peter Smedley gave valuable help throughout with the statistical analyses. We give our thanks also to those who read and commented on the manuscript and in particular to Miss Joyce Baird, Dr Graham Ruddock and Peter Dickson for their encouragement and advice. We acknowledge, too, the support we received throughout from Mrs Ann Symmonds, who carried out her duties as project secretary with skill and patience and who, with Mrs Stephanie Box, was responsible for typing the final manuscript.

B.G.
M.I.R.
July 1983

List of Tables

Chapter One

The Project: Aims and Methods

Why a study of reports?

School reports are the principal formal means of informing parents about the progress of their children in the secondary school. In addition, they implicitly provide parents with other information about a school and its teachers, their values and emphases. With the exception of some special schools, all schools regard reports as a key component in their communications with parents. Within school, too, the report may be important in providing a record of a student's performance across the curriculum, bringing together the views of a range of subject specialists and conveying an overall picture to those responsible for the academic and pastoral welfare of the student. There may be no other record as comprehensive.

Over the years, comment from a variety of sources has indicated concern about the effectiveness of the school report as a means of communicating information about students. In the year before the research which forms the subject of this book was started, the Department of Education and Science in its consultative document *Education in Schools* (1977) drew attention to the variable quality of existing reports and suggested that they should be 'more comprehensive and comprehensible' in order to meet parents' requirements for more information. Other bodies such as the Association of Assistant Mistresses (AAM)[1] and the Home and School Council indicated their concern by publishing recommendations and guidelines for schools and teachers (AAM, 1976; Home and School Council, 1975). In addition some individual writers have been more sharply critical of reporting practices.

---

[1] This association subsequently amalgamated with its male counterpart to form the present Assistant Masters and Mistresses Association (AMMA).

Jackson (1971), for example, reviewing 365 secondary school reports submitted by members of the Advisory Council for Education (ACE) drew attention to what she termed 'their telegraph language', 'inconsistency', and 'negative judgements' and concluded that 'ninety per cent of school reports are bureaucratic form-filling of the most pointless kind'. Later, Woods (1979), using a very different approach, viewed school reports in the light of the 'professionalism' which he considered the key element in understanding teacher activity, and described their function as being 'to insulate and protect teachers and reinforce their power to help to cultivate the impression of detachment and omniscience. . . .' Research conducted at the Foundation, however, indicated that many teachers felt themselves far from omniscient in matters relating to assessment and reporting. In the course of their investigations into mixed ability teaching (Reid *et al.*, 1981) the researchers encountered teachers keenly aware of the problems of effectively communicating information on childrens' performance to parents. They also encountered parents bewildered by both the grouping policies within secondary schools and the assessments they received on reports. For many, the organization of school and the nature of the curriculum had undergone substantial changes since their own schooldays.

The need for effective strategies for informing and communicating with parents has seldom been more apparent. Despite the long-established place of school reports in the home–school communication system, there have been few large-scale, systematic investigations either in this country or abroad concerning the functions that reports in reality fulfil, or the extent of their usefulness to parent, teacher and student. Hence, while the literature on assessment in general, and on specific aspects of assessment such as grading, is extensive, that concerning how assessment information is *mediated* to various audiences – parents, colleagues or pupils – is, by comparison, sparse.

The research

The project, which started in spring 1978, had as its principal aim to investigate current policy and practice relating to reports to parents in a sample of secondary schools. The inquiry sought information from heads, teachers, parents and pupils in an attempt to gain a wide range of perspectives on the reporting process. Survey methods were supplemented as necessary with school visits, and a broad agenda of areas of inquiry was drawn up in the early weeks of the project from two day-long seminars in which groups of heads and advisers drawn from schools and authorities in and around the home counties discussed what they considered the pertinent issues. After this a number of survey tools were developed and these are described in the following paragraphs.

i.   The questionnaire for schools

A questionnaire was devised with two parts; the first, designed for completion by heads, explored the origin of the system of reporting currently in use, its functions within the school, the part played by parents evenings and teachers', parents' and pupils' reactions to the reporting system. Other questions explored the role of the head and collected opinions and biographical information pertinent to the report.

The second stage of the instrument was addressed to the person with overall responsibility for organizing reporting in the school. This was usually a deputy head although in a small minority of cases the head chose to provide the answers. This questionnaire collected basic information about the school, its size, designated status, the age range of its pupils and its organization. Areas explored included the types of report in use and the functions to which they were put, the nature of the assessments they contained, the advice offered about reports to teachers, parents and pupils, the issue and return of reports, administrative details concerned with parents' evenings and aspects of home—school relations. Schools were asked to provide examples of the reports currently in use and any supporting information prepared for teachers or parents. Staff lists were also requested from schools willing to take part in a study of the role of the teacher (*v.* section ii).

The questionnaire was sent to a 20 per cent sample of maintained secondary schools in England and Wales. Secondary schools in this case included all those providing for children between the ages of 11 and 18 years. The sample therefore included schools designated as middle schools, selective and comprehensive schools of all types and sixth form colleges. Altogether, 945 schools were sent the questionnaire and 740 completed it, a response rate of 78 per cent. A 10 per cent sample of special schools, again catering for the secondary age range, was also sent the questionnaire in a slightly modified form. Ninety-seven of these 152 special schools (64 per cent) returned completed questionnaires.

Many heads of school gave reasons for their unwillingness or inability to provide information, and differences were apparent between ordinary and special schools. A number of the non-respondent ordinary schools were in the process of reorganization. Such reorganization was due either to local changes in the secondary provision such as school amalgamations or to a change of head teacher or to some other major restructuring of the school or its reporting system. Although such reorganization was also given as a reason for non-participation by some special schools two other reasons were more common. One was a concentration within their schools on verbal reporting which rendered many of the questions irrelevant; the second was a rejection of an inquiry into reporting practice in special schools due to the nature of their population and the 'technical' and 'confidential' nature of the material.

The respondents from ordinary schools corresponded fairly closely to the national population in terms of school type (Appendix A, Table A1) and school size (Table A2). In the case of special schools, the correspondence between the respondent sample and the total population, in terms of school type, was less close, with ESN(S) schools being over-represented and ESN(M) and hospital schools under-represented.

ii.   *The teacher surveys*

Two kinds of teacher survey were carried out. The first focused on teachers' involvement in reporting during the previous academic year and explored areas such as the numbers of subject and tutorial reports completed for different year groups, the time demands, difficulties encountered by teachers in different subject areas and aspects of the teachers' experience and background. Questions were included on any preparation received in reporting and assessment techniques in either initial or in-service training.

One hundred schools were randomly selected from among those which responded to the questionnaire described in section i and teachers were randomly sampled from the staff lists these schools provided.

The final sample, selected to give approximately one quarter of the teachers in each school, comprised 1,205 teachers.

Individually addressed questionnaires were sent to these teachers via the head who also returned sealed responses to the project. Six hundred and forty-seven teachers completed the questionnaire, a response rate of 54 per cent. The respondent sample included teachers of varying lengths of experience (Table A3). Sixty-nine per cent held posts of responsibility and eight per cent were employed on a part-time basis.

The second type of teacher survey consisted of inquiries specifically focused on a single issue — for example, the workload associated with reporting, parents' evenings, *and* teachers' perceptions of the value of reports. Teachers from various subject areas selected from different types of school and from schools with various reporting systems were invited to write freely on the particular topic. Altogether, over all the mini surveys, some 350 teachers (just under half of those approached) gave more detailed information on selected aspects of reporting.

iii.   *The pupil and parent surveys*

It was considered essential that the research included some study of the two main 'consumers' of the school report: the pupils and parents. How did pupils view their report? Which information did they find useful? Did they consider it accurate and fair? Did they intend to change their behaviour as a result of it?

In order to explore areas such as these, six schools, all comprehensive and mixed, were selected for further surveys. An outline of their characteristics is given in Table A4. Approximately one third of the pupils were selected from each of the year groups from age 11-plus to 15-plus. Where children were grouped by ability (in sets, streams or bands) an attempt was made to balance the different levels of achievement within the school. The project team visited each school in the spring and summer terms of 1980 as soon as was feasible after the school had issued a report. The pupils were given a questionnaire seeking information and reaction to that report and completed questionnaires were received from 2,016 (92 per cent). The remaining eight per cent were absent from school on the day of the survey.

In four of the schools all pupils who were present for the pupil survey were given a further questionnaire to take home for their parents.

In the other two schools the parent questionnaires were issued with the school report. As it was intended to compare parents' views with those of their children, the inclusion of parents was governed by the pupil sample and a few parents responded who could not be 'matched' with pupils, as their children had been absent on the day of the pupil survey. Altogether, responses from 1,374 parents were used in this part of the study – just over two thirds of the parents of the pupil sample.

iv.   Field-based studies

Survey data usually requires amplification and very often in research projects, a questionnaire phase is followed by more intensive, field-based studies. This was the approach adopted in this instance. Schools were visited to clarify and explore issues raised by heads and teachers in their responses to the survey questions. It was thought particularly important to include special schools, middle schools and sixth form colleges in this part of the research, to ensure that any factors specific to their circumstances could be investigated. Finally, a small number of studies was carried out in order to gather more detailed information on certain topics such as the teacher's role in grading and assessment and the involvement of pupils in reporting.

The information from these studies and from the questionnaire surveys is presented as follows. Chapters 2 and 3 map out existing reporting policy and practice: the forms of report in use, how these are selected, what reports contain, what their perceived function is and how they fit in with other forms of communication, both in-school and between the school and parents. Chapter 4 focuses on the demands that producing the report make on the staff of schools and examines the contribution of heads and teachers. Some of the major problems and issues identified by those teaching in schools are dealt with in Chapter 5, while the pupils' views, and those of their parents, are dealt with in Chapters 6 and 7 respectively. Alternative reporting strategies and innovative practice are described in Chapter 8, and Chapter 9 provides an overview of major findings and puts forward a framework for schools wishing to evaluate and revise their system of reporting.

Chapter Two

Content and Function

This chapter sets the scene by describing the types of report being used at present and identifies the originators of the schools' reporting systems. Heads' views on what reports should contain are reported together with an analysis of the content of a sizeable sample of reports sent to the project in the course of its inquiries. The chapter concludes with a review of the functions which heads perceived reports to perform in their schools.

Types of report

The national survey showed that the reporting system in schools was dominated by three main kinds of report, with fairly limited variation within each type. The purpose here is to describe these, which are termed the 'single sheet', the 'report book' and the 'slip report' respectively. Other forms will also be identified although an exploration of the more innovative systems will be delayed until Chapter 8.

The single sheet

An example of a single sheet report is given in Figure 2.1. With this type of report each subject teacher is required to assign a grade or mark and to write their comments in the boxes provided. To cope with the variety of subjects due to option choices, the reports for third, fourth and fifth years often leave the subject spaces unlabelled (Figure 2.2). A section at the bottom of the sheet is completed by the form tutor and frequently includes totals of absence and lateness. A small space is usually allowed for a brief comment and signature

FIRST YEAR REPORT			**COMPREHENSIVE SCHOOL**	

Name_____   Form_____   Date_____

A: Very Good   B: Good   C: Average   D: Below Average   E: Poor

SUBJECT	Course	EXAM	REMARKS	INITIALS
Art				
Drama				
English				
French				
Geography				
History				
Home Economics				
Mathematics				
Metalwork				
Music				
Needlecraft				
Religious Education				
Science				
Woodwork				
Physical Education				
Integrated Studies				
Half Days Absent	Conduct		Punctuality	

_____
                                                        Form Tutor

_____
            Head of Lower School   *Headmaster*

I have seen and read the report on

_____
                                              (Student's Name)

*Signature of Parent/Guardian*_____   Date_____

Figure 2.1:   *A single sheet report*

FOURTH/FIFTH YEAR REPORT		**COMPREHENSIVE SCHOOL**			
Name_____		Form_____		Date_____	
SUBJECT	G.C.E. C.S.E.	EFFORT	REMARKS		INITIALS
English Language					
English Literature					
Mathematics					
Religious Education					
Physical Education					
School Activities and Responsibilities					
Half Days Absent	/	Conduct		Punctuality	

_____   *Form Tutor*

_____ Head of Middle/Upper School _____   *Headmaster*

I, the undersigned, have seen and read the report for

_____ (Student's Name)

*Signature of Parent/Guardian*_____   Date _____

Figure 2.2:   *A single sheet report for the upper school*

Name:_____   Form:_____

Date of this Report:_____

Subject	%	Pos.	Set	Remarks	Master
English					
Mathematics					
French					
Latin					
German/ Social Studies					
Geography					
History					
Biology					
Chemistry					
Physics					
Art					
Music					
Woodwork					
Divinity					

Figure 2.3:   *A page from a typical report book* (actual size 230 x 350 mm)

Position in form: _____ No. in form: _____

Average per cent: _____

Half-days absent: _____ Times late: _____

Merit Marks: _____ Conduct Marks: _____

Detentions: _____

Comment on Physical Education:

Form Master's Comments:

Headmaster's Comments:

Parent's Signature:

Next term begins on:

by the head teacher and head of a larger pastoral unit, such as a house or year.

On many of the reports a small 'key' to the grading is also provided, commonly of the type:

A = Very good   B = Good   C = Average   D = Below average   E=Poor

Most sheets collected in the project required parents to acknowledge receipt of the report and in a few cases space was allowed for parents to return their comments on the report with the acknowledgement. Sheet reports were commonly printed on A4 paper, although some were up to twice this size, and a few were as small as three quarters of A4. Many were printed on NCR (no carbon required or self-carbonized) paper which allowed the second, and in some cases third, copies to be retained within the school record system.

The report book

At its simplest, the report book consists of a series of single sheet reports bound into a cover.

Such reports showed considerable variety in page size and in the number of pages they contained, this being associated with the number of reports issued during the school life of the student and the number of pages allocated to each individual report. This varied from a single side of paper to four sides for each report. Some of the more substantial books were bound, with board covers and linen spines, but more commonly the cover was of light card and occasionally of a low-grade sugar paper.

Page layout closely followed that already described for single sheet reports although lines were more commonly ruled and the space for teacher comments was slightly larger (Figure 2.3). Descriptions of the assessment system were usually printed inside the cover or on the first page and approximated to the fuller descriptions found among the single sheet reports. Because the report book moved backwards and forwards between school and home the cover usually carried an exhortation to take care of it and statements reminding students and parents that the report book was the property of the school were quite common.

The slip report

Reports of this type showed a marked departure from those already described. They consisted of a series of pages, one or more of which might be completed by each teacher, the whole series then being stapled together within a thin card cover (Figures 2.4 and 2.5). A common size for this type of report was one third of an A4 page but, again, there was considerable variation, with the smallest providing only marginally more space for teacher comment than that offered by single sheet or book reports, while the largest approached A4 in size.

In its simplest form each slip had space for the student's name and comments by the subject teacher. More complex examples included boxes for assessment grades and spaces for an array of information: form, set, number in set, date, examination mark and so on. On rare examples the subject name was printed and there were occasionally subject-specific page layouts to cope with — for example, the absence of grades in physical education or the provision of grades only in mathematics.

Separate slips were included for the form tutor and these were sometimes supplemented by a further slip completed by the head of year or house or by the head of lower, middle or upper school.

A description of the grading system was often given on the inside cover or on a further slip. In some examples this page provided parents with an account of the total number of pages contained in the report, ensuring that no pages could be removed between school and home. Many had a section for the parent to sign and return to school and a number gave parents a full page on which to write a response to the report. Most examples of slip reports were printed on NCR paper, often in blue, possibly to minimize the impact of the blue tinge commonly observable with NCR paper.

Other types of report

The remaining written reports which schools sent the project came into one of two categories. The first of these resembled the single sheet report but generally contained no subdivisions, consisting of a headed page upon which teachers could write at length. Occasionally up to one third of the available space was allocated to the form tutor's report. These were termed 'letter reports' by the project.

Figure 2.4:   *A slip report* (a)

HEADMASTER'S COMMENT:	PARENT'S COMMENT:

FORM TEACHER'S REPORT

Name... Age.............. Form............... Date........................

SUBJECT REPORT

Name... Subject.. Form/Set..............

Grades Attainment........................... Effort...............

(Grade A is highest grade, grade E the lowest)   Signed...

EXPLANATION OF GRADES USED IN THIS REPORT

FOURTH AND EXAMINATION YEARS

ATTAINMENT GRADES

Grades A—E are used to indicate a pupil's performance relative to public examinations (G.C.E., C.S.E., R.S.A., etc.)

A suggests a very good G.C.E. performance; B a performance likely to produce a pass in G.C.E. or Grade 1 C.S.E.; C a grade 2—4 in C.S.E.; D a grade 5 in C.S.E.; and E a C.S.E. unclassified result.

EFFORT GRADES

Effort is graded A — Excellent. B — Good. C — Satisfactory. D — Poor.
E — Extremely Poor.

Figure 2.5:   *A slip report* (b)

FORM TEACHER'S REPORT

Name...

| Attendance |
| Punctuality |

....
Form Teacher.

SUBJECT REPORT FOR...

Name.. Form .... Set ....

| ATTAINMENT |
| EFFORT |

Signature...

HEADMASTER'S & TUTOR'S REPORT

Name...

....
Tutor.

....
Headmaster.

The second category consisted of a single piece of paper or light card providing a list of subjects together with boxes in which to enter assessments. Such a report, because it contained no space for teacher comment, was termed a 'grade card' and was often used to provide an interim report to parents.

While just over half the schools used the same format for all years, 28 per cent had two different reports and a fifth used up to nine forms of layout. The type of report being used in different year groups is given in Table 2.1.

Table 2.1: The type of report in use in different years

| Type of report | Years | | | | | | |
	1 %	2 %	3 %	4 %	5 %	6 %	7 %
Slips	39	41	44	48	48	56	56
Books	14	13	12	12	13	9	9
Sheets	43	42	40	38	37	32	33
Letter reports	2	1	1	—	1	1	1
Others†	3	3	3	3	2	2	1
Totals	101††	100	100	101††	101††	100	100

† Major component grade cards.
†† Rounding error.

Slips and single sheet reports were by far the most commonly used types of report in all years, with the use of slip systems increasing as pupils got older.

Choosing the reporting system

Table 2.2 shows the originators of the current system of reporting in the schools surveyed.

In ordinary schools the most common method of establishing the reporting system was through a working party in combination with the head teacher. Table 2.2 shows that heads were involved in a major way in the selection of the reporting system in 84 per cent of the ordinary schools and were solely responsible in 28 per cent. The situation

Table 2.2: The originator(s) of the schools' reporting system

Originator	Ordinary schools (N = 740)		Special schools (N = 97)	
	N	%	N	%
Head teacher	195	28	45	57
Another member of staff, e.g. deputy head	12	2	2	3
Senior members of staff	60	8	1	1
Staff working party	46	7	2	3
Combination of the head teacher with a working party†	393	56	29	37
Totals	706	101††	79	101††
'Don't know' responses and non-respondents	34		18	

† A minority involved senior members of staff, the head teacher and
 a working party.
†† Rounding error.

in special schools showed even greater involvement of the head, who was the sole originator in 57 per cent of the schools and had some involvement in 94 per cent.

Where the head had played the major role in selecting the report, in nine out of ten cases staff had been consulted. In these and in other schools, however, there had been little consultation with any other groups; parents, governors and students were rarely recorded as being involved in discussions (Table 2.3).

The content of the report

In their questionnaire heads were asked to give their views about what should appear on a report and a five-point scale ranging from 'essential to include' to 'should not appear' was used to rate the importance of a number of items (Table A5). Subject and pastoral comments were considered essential by over 90 per cent of heads; these are, traditionally, of course, what the report is all about. Among the items considered essential by over two thirds of heads were:

Table 2.3: Those involved in discussions on choosing the report
(ordinary and special schools)

	Ordinary schools (N = 740)		Special schools (N=97)	
	N	%	N	%
Members of staff	662	90	78	80
Parents	71	10	13	13
Governors	67	9	5	5
Students	10	1	1	1
No discussions	33	4	6	6
Information not available	38	5	1	1

an attendance total; comments (for each subject) on attainment, progress, effort, attitude and behaviour; and grades for attainment and effort.

Other items which received general support (i.e. they were rated as being either 'essential' or 'of moderate value' by over two thirds or more respondents) were:

comment on attendance and punctuality; lateness total; record of extra-curricular activities; space for parental comment; comment on homework, comment on personal development, subject examination grades; a summary of subject reports; and a record of any commendations or merits received.

Items which heads were generally not in favour of including were:

class position (rejected by 72 per cent); subject position; and examination position.

Comment by the student also received little support, with only 11 per cent of heads expressing favourable attitudes and 44 per cent voicing negative views towards it. A large proportion (36 per cent) of heads, however, recorded a response in the 'uncertain' category to this item – presumably because they had no experience of this kind of student participation and felt unable to formulate an opinion as to its merits.

There were, as is apparent from Table A5, some items on which heads were widely divided in their views and relatively large numbers made use of the opportunity to give 'uncertain' as their response. All of these items concerned grading and included among them were grades for behaviour/conduct; personal development; homework; and progress. The inclusion of a grade predictive of GCE or CSE results was supported by 47 per cent of heads and rejected by 25 per cent, with 15 per cent 'uncertain'.

The various headings of the reports which the schools sent as examples were inspected to get some idea of what the content was in practice. As noted earlier, almost half the schools were using more than one report format and altogether 1,321 examples of reports were received from 706 of the ordinary schools. Attendance total, rated an essential item by 67 per cent of heads, was in fact allocated a headed space on 68 per cent of the reports inspected, and 47 per cent also had space for a comment on punctuality — an item deemed essential by 25 per cent of heads. Space for attainment/achievement grades appeared on 60 per cent of reports inspected, and for effort grades on 53 per cent. The percentages of heads stating on their questionnaires that attainment and effort grades were included on reports in their schools were considerably higher (90 and 63 per cent respectively) and this apparent discrepancy in the evidence may be explained by the fact that schools with, say, one report format for younger pupils and another for more senior students, might include such grades only on the latter. A very small percentage of the reports allocated space for attitude/behaviour/conduct grades (eight per cent), homework grades (seven per cent) and grades for progress (two per cent) and personal qualities such as industry and appearance (two per cent).

Heads did not generally support the inclusion of form or examination position and neither was allocated space on more than ten per cent of reports. Most of the reports, however, gave an indication of the group or set to which the student was allocated but descriptions of the band, stream or set in which the student was placed were rare (five per cent of reports) as were details of the group's size (12 per cent). Indications of the average age of the year group were similarly infrequent (eight per cent) as were indications of the level of the course being undertaken by pupils in their fourth and fifth years. Over half did, however, provide a key to explain the grading system, with a further 28 per cent offering a detailed explanation of the basis for the grades. The distribution of grades was explained on five per cent of the reports.

A number of the items which heads had considered essential for inclusion received no headed space allocation on the report. Extra-curricular activities, for example, an essential item for 60 per cent of heads, appeared as a heading on only 19 per cent of the reports inspected. Similarly space for comment on attitude, behaviour and conduct, again deemed essential by well over two thirds of heads, was given headed space for comment on only 11 per cent of reports, while space for comment specifically on personal qualities was allocated in only two per cent of cases. The assumption, of course, must be that such items were covered in the comments of the subject teachers and pastoral tutors. There clearly, however, is a danger that those areas which present the greatest challenge to assessment skills, and which many argue are not susceptible to techniques such as grading, may fail to receive comment if no space is made specifically available for it and if checks are not carried out to ensure that they have been covered.

Several further points emerged from the inspection of the sample of reports. First, there were indications of considerable variation in practice concerning the production and retention of a copy of the report by schools. Thirty-eight per cent of the reports provided by schools used NCR paper (self-carbonized or no carbon required), a further six per cent required the use of carbon paper, two per cent required the teacher to make either a full or a summary copy and six per cent requested that parents return the original for storage in the school until the leaving age was reached. The remaining reports provided no obvious school copy although almost 80 per cent of heads indicated in their questionnaire responses that a copy was retained.

Second, where reports contained subject headings, the space allocated to each subject was the same in three out of four cases. Where differences among subjects occurred, English, mathematics and science most usually had a larger space allocation than other subjects. Also, the space allowed for pastoral comment was larger on two thirds of the reports examined. Such pastoral comment was most commonly provided by the form tutor, although in a small proportion of schools (seven per cent) space was provided for the head of house or head of year to comment and three per cent included space for the head of upper, middle and lower school. Two thirds of reports allocated space for a comment by the head and in a further fifth, space was available for the head's signature.

Sixty per cent of the reports required a parental signature either on the report itself or on a tear-off portion of the report and seven per cent conveyed an invitation to a subsequent parents' evening. Five of the 1,321 reports included a space for student self-assessment. Finally, despite the often-stated view that the school report is a confidential document, only six per cent of reports carried a statement to this effect.

School differences in the type and content of reports

The sample included sixth form colleges, middle and special schools. While some principals of the sixth form colleges considered that since their students were approaching adulthood, the reports should be addressed to them, others thought this inappropriate within the context of 'a school'. Concerning middle schools, where these had derived from primary origins and had staff with primary teaching experience, the reports tended to be less subject-dominated. No statistically significant differences emerged, however, in either the type or content of the reports of all middle schools as compared with other secondary schools, nor between sixth form colleges and other secondary schools.

Special schools made less frequent use of the written report. Some heads wrote of the problem of raising false expectations: 'It is difficult sometimes to report the truth . . . unless words are carefully chosen they can give parents of handicapped children undue hope'. Others, by contrast, were concerned about the potentially depressing effect which a written report might have on both pupil and parent, and pointed out the extremely emotional nature of the relationship between parents and their handicapped child and also the relatively high probability that the handicap was present in the parent too. Despite these points, the importance of frankness and honesty in dealings with parents was stressed by the heads of a number of schools catering for both the physically and intellectually impaired. Examples were also found of schools involved in all aspects of special provision which were able to produce written reports, apparently without the disadvantages described above.

A factor which may have caused difficulties in reporting was the absence of a formalized system of records, noted in some of the special schools visited. Formal recording procedures for assessments were considered unnecessary by some heads because of the small number of staff and the frequency with which they met. In other schools, evidence was found of a wide range of recorded assessments, many of which were clearly of potential interest and value to parents, but which were rarely made available to them.

The functions of the reporting systems

Heads were asked to describe the major functions performed by the reporting system in their schools. Their responses focused on a fairly limited number of processes or activities which were performed by reports and identified the audiences to whom the reports were considered to be of value. Only occasionally were different audiences identified as requiring essentially different treatments.

The most frequent function identified was the apparently simple one of conveying information to parents and very few head teachers carried their analysis on to 'second order' functions such as pupil motivation, parent involvement, teacher self-awareness and the improvement of school performance.

At its lowest level, preparing the report was identified as 'formalizing record-keeping' and the report's function was to render an account of a pupil's performance. In some cases this function was expressed briefly, e.g. 'communication of academic performance'. In others both the function of the report and its intended audience were specified in more detail, for example:

(1) Inform parents of academic attainment.
(2) Inform parents of effort in work.
(3) Inform parents of attitude of student in classroom.
(4) Inform parents of games and societies achievement.
(5) Provide a school record.
(6) Provide basis for parents' evening.
(7) Provide basis for staff to formalise record after exams.

A few head teachers saw themselves and their deputies as part of the potential audience: '(The report) gives valuable information on staff attitudes'; 'Gives head teacher regular feedback on the work of the school.'

Others considered teachers as one of the audiences, where the report's function was to inform staff and aid their professional development. A noteworthy point was that many heads did not include students among the report's intended audience.

Although informing was so commonly identified as a prime function of the report, not all forms of information about pupils were conveyed to the parents. In many schools, for example, additional information was added to the school's copy of the report, or to the record card or collected by the school in other records which were not made available to the parents. Most typically this information included raw scores or marks, examination marks and class, set and year positions. In a few schools *all* marks and grades were considered to be for internal school use only.

A number of heads specifically excluded potential employers from the report's audience on the grounds that the report was a confidential document for parents — 'They (i.e. the reports) are for internal use and to help students to remedy problems, not for future employers.' There were, however, a small number of heads who considered that 'good' reports might effectively be used to support job applications.

A group of heads saw the major function of the report to be the bringing about of greater involvement of the pupils, the parents and the staff. Greater effort from the student might come about through parental pressure or through shame:

> We do find that all-round poor comments cause even the weakest of parents to put some pressure on their off-spring! In most cases, pupils themselves respond to bad reports and endeavour to gain better next time — it seems to shatter them to see their known faults in writing.

In more positive terms the report was identified as a means of motivation or incentive for pupils by 'helping the pupil to form a self image and encouraging the pupil to correct mistakes'. Two further heads emphasized encouragement as follows:

> Its (the report's) main functions, I suppose, should be the encouragement and guidance of the pupil and to enable parents to form a balanced view of what is happening to the child at school and how he is reacting academically, socially and culturally.

> (The report is) . . . a way of giving each child dignity (it is worth writing about), encouragement, praise, helpful criticism and advice and therefore promoting a useful dialogue between teacher and parent, teacher and pupil, teacher and teacher and parent and child.

A number of head teachers emphasized the place of the report in enhancing an open relationship between parents and the school. Several pointed out that the report was only the precursor to further discussions with parents:

> Reports are a routine method of reminding parents of our mutual responsibilities and are followed by a specific invitation to come and discuss progress.

Some of the heads' replies reiterated that the report must be seen in its context as merely one aspect of the whole system of pastoral care and parental involvement in education. In cases where parents had little contact with the school, however, the report was sometimes the *only* link between school and home.

Apart from an increased emphasis upon the value of direct parent–teacher contact and a widening of the possible audience to include educational psychologists, school nurses, medical practitioners and physiotherapists, head teachers in special schools differed little from those in ordinary schools in their conception of school reports. The heads of those special schools which provided written reports described their functions as being to provide parents with a regular progress report, and stimulate them to make contact with the school, motivate pupils ('getting a good report is a goal for children'), provide heads with an overview of pupils' progress and enable teachers to monitor their teaching performance in the light of how pupils were faring.

From the various head teachers' replies, then, reporting could be seen to have three objectives: accounting or informing, changing pupils' attitudes and influencing their performance, and involving the recipients in the process of education. When one considers that these objectives coexisted and frequently involved a variety of audiences – heads and teachers, pupils and parents – the extent of the complexity of reporting becomes apparent.

Summary

The heads of the schools surveyed clearly considered that the choice of their school's reporting system was a matter in which they should be involved, and a sizeable proportion (over a quarter in the case of ordinary schools and more than a half of special school heads) assumed the major responsibility for this task themselves. While in the majority of ordinary schools, other staff shared the responsibility for choosing the reporting system with the head, our evidence suggests that parents, governors and students were involved relatively infrequently. If the parent and pupil be viewed as the major consumers, it seems that schools have a long way to go before any degree of consumer choice is realized.

Two types of report — the single sheet and the report slip — were by far the most commonly used in schools, with slip systems being found increasingly among older year groups. Nearly half the schools used more than one type of report, thereby indicating a realization of the need to cater for different needs at different stages. Schools which catered for a younger (middle schools) or older (sixth form colleges) group of pupils, however, did not differ from other schools in the type or content of their reports. The particular difficulties associated with written reports in special schools were noted.

There was widespread agreement among heads over which items were essential on a report; these included an attendance total, pastoral comment, comments on attainment, progress, effort and attitude and behaviour in each subject and grades for attainment and effort. Others, such as lateness total, record of extra-curricular activities, space for parental comment were also widely endorsed. There was fairly broad rejection of including an indication of a child's position in the class, or his position in subject classwork or examinations. Many heads also rejected the inclusion of any student comment on the report although a sizeable number were unprepared to commit themselves on this issue. Inspection of sample reports sent in to the project indicated that a number of areas which heads considered merited comment, received no headed space allocation on the report form. Often these related to attitude, behaviour or conduct. Attention was drawn to the danger of such important aspects of a child's development at schools being ignored on the report, if teachers were not carefully briefed as to the need for their inclusion. Schools must also consider the possibility of areas which they clearly deem important, such as extra-curricular activities, being devalued in the eyes of parent, pupil and teacher because they receive no allocated space.

School reports fulfil a number of functions for several audiences. Informing parents of pupils' progress was, as might be expected, that most commonly recorded by heads, but analysis of their comments revealed that the report's function could extend beyond this, to changing pupils' attitudes and performance and involving parents in the educational process. The report's function emerged then as being one of *informing, motivating* and *involving* — and its audience might be seen as including heads and teachers as well as parents and pupils.

Chapter Three

Organization and Context

The report is one of a number of means which schools have for recording and passing on information about pupils. In the following section, the place of the report in the contexts of other in-school pupil records and of other means of communicating with parents is considered. As the timing of reports may be associated with the purposes for which they can be used, we begin by describing the yearly reporting cycle in the schools surveyed.

Schools' reporting cycles

The number of reports each year

Over half the ordinary schools provided two reports annually in years one to four and in year six, with most of the remaining schools supplying a single annual report. A very few schools (six) issued two reports each term, in the first three years. In the two years in which large numbers of students were leaving school, years five and seven, two thirds of the schools produced a single report, with the remaining schools providing two reports for those years. As noted in Chapter 2, special schools differed from ordinary schools in their use of written reports. Less than one per cent of the ordinary schools (six) produced no written reports compared with 28 per cent of the special schools. Differences were also apparent in the number of reports which ordinary and special schools issued each year (Appendix A, Table A6). Over three quarters of the special schools providing written reports produced a single report each year and this showed minimal variation between pupils of different ages. Very few special schools (seven per cent or fewer in each year group) provided three written reports — i.e. one for each school term.

Time of issue

Although there were some variations between the times in the school year that reports were issued for different year groups (Table 3.1) much reporting activity took place in the summer term and most of this was concentrated at the very end of the academic year. Special schools displayed a similar pattern with the practice of issuing a single annual report at the end of the summer term appearing even more frequently.

Table 3.1: Times of report issue in different year groups
(ordinary schools)

	Year group						
	Year 1	Year 2	Year 3	Year 4	Year 5	Year 6	Year 7
(Number of schools:†)	(605)	(649)	(615)	(602)	(602)	(380)	(380)
	%	%	%	%	%	%	%
Autumn term							
Early††	5	3	3	3	5	3	3
Late††	38	27	25	26	26	26	20
No report issued	57	70	72	71	69	71	77
Spring term							
Early	28	31	36	31	56	47	53
Late	15	18	34	21	23	21	29
No report issued	57	51	30	48	21	32	18
Summer term							
Early	10	12	9	10	6	9	5
Late	84	83	66	81	21	76	21
No report issued	6	5	25	9	73	15	74

† Thirteen schools did not provide information on the time reports were issued.
†† Early issue takes place before half term and late issue after half term.

A number of head teachers drew attention to specific age- or year-group-related needs in terms of reporting and these included the following:

(a) A need for reassurance on the part of both parents and pupils soon after transfer to the secondary school.
(b) The need for a report in the middle of the third year to aid the selection of appropriate 'options' to be taken in fourth and fifth years.

(c) The need for early to mid-year reports in the fifth and seventh years to clarify entry to public examinations.

The information provided by the sample schools indicated that the standard 'intake' year (first year) received greater attention than other year groups in the autumn term although only 43 per cent of the schools provided a report for their first-year pupils in that term, and very few (28 in all) issued a report in the early part of the term.

Pupils in the third, fifth, sixth and seventh years received a spring term report much more commonly than did other year groups, reflecting schools' response to pupils' need for information at major decision points. End-of-year reports were less common in years five and seven, with nearly four fifths of the schools not issuing reports at this time.

Although a number of head teachers also identified a need for early 'settling-in reports' at the beginning of the fourth and sixth year to reassure parents and pupils that the transfer to a new mode of working had been successfully achieved, very few instances of these were found.

The most commonly used method of conveying reports to parents was for students to take them home. Increased postal charges in recent years has almost irradicated the posted report in ordinary schools although reports were still posted in 25 per cent of the special schools, a reflection of both the residential nature of some of the institutions and of the increased risk of loss by some of the students. In early discussions the team found that many head teachers had fears that a proportion of the reports sent home with students did not reach their destination, and this was one reason why a number (seven per cent of those in ordinary schools and five per cent of special) of head teachers issued reports at parents' evenings, and other were considering the introduction of this procedure. In some cases where it had been introduced, parents not attending the parents' evening were not provided with a report and this is discussed further in Chapter 7.

Other methods of communicating with parents

Most of the schools used other means as well as the report to communicate with parents about the progress of their children and about school policy and practice.

The first opportunity that schools have to provide information for parents is by means of a school prospectus for 'new' parents, and this is usually supplemented by a parents' evening. Despite guidelines laid down by the then Secretary of State for Education (*A New Partnership for our Schools*, HMSO, 1978) basic information was still by no means universally provided, with some 13 per cent of the ordinary schools in the sample not producing a prospectus. Information directly relevant to the reporting process, while occurring in over half the ordinary schools with prospectuses (Table 3.2), was seldom more than a statement of when reports might be issued.

Table 3.2: Information relevant to reporting in the school prospectus

(a) Schools with prospectuses

	Ordinary schools		Special schools	
	N	%	N	%
Prospectus	640	87	44	45
No prospectus	96	13	52	54
Non-respondents	4	1	1	1
Total	740	101††	97	100

(b) Information included in prospectus†

Information on	Ordinary schools %	Special schools %
The report system	57	13
Assessment procedures	24	10
Interpretation of grades/marks	19	3

† Schools may provide information on more than one area.
†† Rounding error.

Few schools provided information on assessment procedures, or on the interpretation of grades and marks in their prospectus. Both these areas are obviously closely related with reporting and the problems parents encountered with them will be explored in Chapter 7.

Information on matters such as the organization of the school, the nature of the courses provided, the homework requirement and how it would be marked, the role of internal school examinations and the nature and purpose of remedial withdrawal was frequently absent. Where such information was given it was sometimes phrased in language more suitable for teachers. School newsletters were referred to in a number of documents with the suggestion that they would provide information when there was a 'need to know'. Such approaches have been the subject of recent research elsewhere (see Bastiani, 1980); clearly they have the potential to overcome some of the problems of the prospectus which may easily be lost or forgotten and the information which it contains may quickly become outdated.

Fewer special schools provided a prospectus (Table 3.2) and this was less likely to contain information related to reporting. Discussions with special school head teachers confirmed that many did not consider that this type of information was necessary. Most interviews were conducted in the year following the publication of *Special Educational Needs* (the Warnock Report) which had drawn attention to the importance for such schools to enter into a dialogue with parents. Clearly, the prospectus was not seen as an appropriate vehicle for such dialogue by many special school heads.

Other forms of written communication with parents found in ordinary schools included letters recording extremes of achievement and information relating to critical decision points such as the selection of options in the third year, or entry to public examinations. Schools varied considerably in their procedures for communicating with parents over these matters but dominant were letters, specially prepared booklets and parent—teacher discussions. As noted earlier, the timing of third- and fifth-year reports was arranged in a number of schools to provide information at the time when choices were to be made.

Parents' evenings were a major feature of home—school communication in most schools and these are explored fully in Chapter 7. Apart from these, one of the most commonly recorded means of home—school communication was visits to the school by parents. Heads pointed out that although every effort was made to see parents it was normally expected that they would initially contact the school to make an appointment. Instances were found of schools where parents were cautioned in the prospectus to make use of the facility to visit the school only in emergencies.

Many examples, however, were found of schools making considerable efforts to communicate with parents. Students' progress was frequently discussed with parents over the telephone and most staff were involved occasionally in home visiting, although visits by senior staff were much more common. A small number of schools also made use of their educational welfare officer in this way and a smaller group still had access to the services of a school social worker or a home—school liaison officer. One school, somewhat eccentrically placed in its catchment area, held regular off-site surgeries taking advantage of the more appropriately placed primary schools.

A community school visited by the team provided an example of what could develop when the school became a major community focus offering contact with teaching staff in social and recreational settings. In that context the problems were changed from the more usual ones occurring in parental contacts to those which demanded an extension of the staff's professional role in order to provide a wide variety of services — social, advisory and counselling. Other head teachers confirmed the 'spin-off' benefits to be accrued from the opportunity for staff—parent contact in more unconventional settings.

The report in the context of the school

Heads were asked to indicate those areas where school reports made a *major* contribution to the life of the school. As might be expected, Table 3.3 indicates that, in the view of head teachers, its most important role was in home—school relations although this was identified as less important in special schools. Over half the ordinary schools identified reports as making a major contribution to the academic work of the school and to the pastoral care system, and almost as many recorded a contribution to careers guidance.

Heads wrote of their value as being 'self-evident', of reports being an 'integral part of school policy' and forming 'a major link at all times'. Others expressed the view that 'all written information is vital in a large school', recording the frequent use of such information at departmental and other meetings, and as an important factor in the choice of subjects and in the preparation of testimonials.

Not all heads, however, were convinced of their importance: 'School reports keep parents *minimally* in touch with what happens or may happen in school. They are *not* the source of assessment and opinions produced and used internally.' Information concerning all internal and external reports produced within the school was gathered to

Table 3.3: Areas of school life where the report made a major
contribution

Areas contributed to†	Ordinary schools (N = 740) %	Special schools (N = 97) %
Home—school relations	75	53
Academic work	58	30
Pastoral care	52	20
Careers guidance	48	32
Student placement, etc.	40	22

† Schools were able to indicate more than one area.

provide a context for the report produced for parents. It was clear
that reports for parents were but one of a wide range of documents
provided by schools for a number of internal and external audiences.
Within the school, for example, daily reports or special or occasional
reports might be made on children as required and nearly two thirds
of the ordinary schools had assessment or grade sheets. Reports for
external audiences included the UCCA reports for university entrance
and reports for the careers, psychological and probationary services.

The extent to which heads considered schools routinely used internal
and external reports as a focus for staff discussion on various issues
is shown in Table 3.4. This shows that in a substantial proportion of
schools reports to parents had an established role in discussions relating
to matters such as settling in from other schools, allocation to and
transfer between sets and streams, transfer to further and higher
education, career choice, academic performance, option choice, examination entry and behaviour difficulties. But in each area, internal
reports provided the material for teacher discussions in more schools
than did the report to parents, and 14 per cent of schools made no
use of reports in such discussions. Further, evidence from the teacher
sample indicated that while nearly two thirds of the 647 teachers
used the report as an occasional focus for discussion with colleagues,
very few used them frequently. One teacher gave the explanation that
'records and reports are always done too hastily . . . more useful is
the day-to-day build-up of knowledge about pupils' work and
behaviour.' Where used, school reports most frequently featured
in discussions about placement of students, promotions and demotions

within the set structure, and the allocation of pupils to option groups. As might be expected, careers and pastoral staff made more frequent use of reports than other teachers.

Table 3.4: Routine use of internal and external reports as a focus
for staff discussion (ordinary schools)

Matter under discussion†	Internal reports	Reports for parents
	% schools (N = 740)	
Settling in from other schools	53	49
Set or stream changes	61	42
Academic performance	67	55
Transfer to other schools	53	45
Selection of option subjects	58	50
Behaviour difficulties	78	47
External examinations entry††	53	41
Transfer to sixth form††	45	33
Transfer to further/higher education††	51	37
Career choice††	60	45
Not routinely used for staff discussions	6	14

† Schools may use the report(s) for discussions concerning more than one matter.
†† Percentages for these items are expressed as a percentage of those schools containing students older than 15 years.

The comments of the teacher quoted above related not just to reports, but to other school records. Relatively few (one third) of the teachers reported having made reference to the school record card in the previous year, most commonly to assist in the production of reports for potential employers or institutions for further and higher education, or where exceptional problems of ill-health or mis-behaviour arose. Internal record cards were seldom used in the preparation of reports to parents or as a basis for discussions with them. In some cases teachers' access to records was restricted to certain members of staff and in others, where more general access was offered, records were described which contained 'sealed envelopes' which 'we are not allowed to open'. Even where access was unrestricted, however, there was evidence of 'teacher-rejection':

I dislike school report cards. The use of A, B, C, D, E gradings for undefined personality attributes such as honesty, perseverance and conscientiousness is very suspect.

This raises wider problems relating to assessment which will be pursued in Chapter 5.

Summary and discussion

The majority of ordinary schools produced two reports annually for years one to four and year six, with a sizeable minority (over a third) opting for a single annual report in these year groups. A different pattern emerged in years five and seven, where two thirds of schools issued one report only. Over a quarter of the special schools issued no written reports and over three quarters of those which did produced an annual report for each year group. The tendency for schools to produce a report at the end of the summer term was noted (less common in the case of fifth- and seventh-year pupils) and this practice merits examination, particularly in those schools where the aim of reports is to motivate pupils. A new academic year frequently brings a change of teacher, sometimes changes of subjects. The usefulness of a report concerned with a situation which no longer exists should be questioned. Even where the context remains the same, as is frequently the case at the end of year four, a long intervening vacation must reduce the chance of reports being acted on by pupils.

There was evidence of schools timing the issue of reports to correspond with important choice points for the pupil; hence spring term reports were much more common in years three, five, six and seven than in other year groups. A number of heads also drew attention to the need for 'settling-in' reports for pupils soon after transfer to secondary school; fewer than half the schools, however, produced a report for pupils in the autumn term and only five per cent issued one in the first half of term. Clearly, the timing of the issue of reports must be considered alongside the purposes it is hoped they fulfil.

The report has been considered in this chapter in the context of other methods of communicating with parents — e.g. prospectuses (found in most ordinary schools but in less than half of special schools), home visits, visits to school by parents, parents' evenings, and other forms of written communication such as newsletters, and documents prepared for specific purposes such as third-year option choices. Three quarters of heads of ordinary schools considered that reports made a major contribution to home–school relations, a view shared by just over half the heads of special schools, and substantial proportions also attributed to them major contributions to the academic, pastoral and careers work in their schools. Of interest, however, is that whereas reports are routinely used in staff discussions on a range of issues – including academic performance, transfer to other schools, selection of options, careers choice – internal records, such as assessment or grade sheets/cards of special daily or occasional reports, were more frequently used for every issue listed in Table 3.4. For example, for behavioural difficulties, 78 per cent of schools routinely used internal reports as a basis for staff discussion as compared with 47 per cent of schools using the report to parents for this purpose. Hence, while the report for parents has a function as an in-school document, teachers more usually use other records to inform their discussion about pupils. Clearly, many schools use both the parental report and internal records for important issues relating to the academic and pastoral welfare of pupils and this raises questions concerning the extent to which these complement each other, the extent to which one duplicates the other and, most important, what information is contained on school records which is not made available to parents and why. Sinister assumptions should be avoided here; the most common form of internal record was the special or occasional report found in 80 per cent of ordinary schools and 62 per cent of special schools. It is not difficult to understand why, when a behavioural difficulty crops up, such internal reports, compiled for a clearly defined purpose at a particular critical time are more relevant and useful than the general-purpose parental report issued probably at the end of a summer term. Attention should rather focus on any information which is *routinely* gathered on pupils and which is excluded from the school report. A detailed analysis of the content of school records was outside the scope of this research; clearly it is an area which would repay study.

Chapter Four

School Staff and the Time Demands of Reporting

Reporting is a demanding business — demanding of skill, time and commitment. In the sections which follow we examine what reporting means in term of the workload it places on teachers, starting with the head.

Heads' involvement in teaching and reporting

In our initial discussions with teachers a number had suggested that some of the problems that arose for teachers were not recognized by their head because they were no longer involved in writing school reports. In fact, over two thirds (68 per cent) of head teachers in ordinary schools completed reports for classes which they taught. The proportion of special school head teachers who were involved in teaching and reporting was somewhat lower (45 per cent). Replies from heads in both special and ordinary schools indicated that similar proportions of heads taught and reported on pupils in each year group and many did so for more than one.

While many heads were, then, themselves involved in report writing, a number saw the need to delegate the responsibility for organizing, coordinating or supervising the reporting procedures in their schools. Table 4.1 indicates that only a quarter of the heads in ordinary schools retained these responsibilities, although the proportion in special schools was very much higher (86 per cent). The table highlights the importance of the part played by the senior pastoral staff and, to a lesser extent, the deputy head, in ordinary schools.

Another aspect of reporting which a head teacher may delegate is that of checking reports before they are issued. Such a check was carried

Table 4.1: Responsibility for the organization, coordination and
supervision of the reporting system

Person responsible	Ordinary schools (N = 740) %	Special schools (N = 97) %
Head teacher	26	86
Deputy head teacher	21	9
Senior pastoral staff		
(e.g. head of year/house)	40	3
Senior academic staff		
(e.g. heads of faculty)	1	–
Combination of above	11	1
Such organization		
considered unnecessary	2	1
Totals	101†	100
Missing cases	62	28

† Rounding error.

out in 95 per cent of ordinary schools and 86 per cent of special schools
and despite the large numbers of reports in some of the ordinary
schools two thirds of the heads themselves checked reports (Table 4.2),
although in no school was the head carrying out the only check. Again,
senior pastoral staff were commonly involved, as were form tutors and
deputy heads. In some schools reports were checked by as many as
three people.

Heads frequently recorded their commitment to involvement in all
aspects of reporting, and one explained his part in the checking process
as follows:

Staff take a variety of attitudes to reporting. It is therefore essential
that the Head checks every report for serious anomalies and signs.
Personally I can see no other way which would do justice to the
educative process for which I am responsible to the school community.

Table 4.2: Staff involvement in checking reports

Staff member involved†	Ordinary schools (N = 740) %	Special schools (N = 97) %
Head	68	90
Deputy head	24	8
Senior pastoral staff	60	2
Form tutor	36	—
Subject teacher	7	—
No formal checking of reports	5	14
Missing cases/no written reports	37	35

† Reports may be checked by more than one member of staff.

Many heads, however, limited the extent to which they could become involved:

> I used to write a comment on all reports. As the school grew larger I had to give this up but I read and checked them all. In recent years I have found time to read only a small sample. I very much regret this; it is a real loss of contact with the mainstream of the school's work.

The sample of reports seen was, in one or two cases, a 'random' one but more commonly house or year tutors were asked to select examples of both 'good' and 'bad' reports for further comment by the head teacher.

Sixty per cent of the ordinary schools in the sample gave parents the opportunity to make a written reply to the report. Table 4.3 shows that few head teachers in ordinary schools dealt with parents' replies, which were mainly handled by the form tutor. In special schools, however, where it was much less common for parents to be given the chance to reply, the majority of heads continued to play a major part in reading the parental replies.

Heads were asked to estimate the amount of time they spent on reporting. The difficulties inherent in questions such as this are apparent and almost a quarter of head teachers found it impossible to answer.

Table 4.3: Staff involved in reading parental replies to
school reports

Staff member	Ordinary schools (N = 450) %	Special schools (N = 25) %
Head	5	65
Deputy head	1	
Senior pastoral staff	20	4
Form tutor	74	30
Totals	100	99†
Missing cases	9	1

† Rounding error.

Those completing the item frequently added riders suggesting caution
in any interpretation of the figures provided. As might be expected,
considerable variation was found among heads who responded, with
approximately half estimating that their work with reports had occupied
the equivalent of one full week or less in the previous year. Those recording the highest involvement estimated the work was equivalent to
over 2½ school weeks (nine per cent of head teachers in ordinary
schools and five per cent of heads in special schools).

The teachers' contribution

The 647 teachers sampled (Chapter 1) represented all the major teaching disciplines and showed a wide variation in the length of teaching
experience within their present school, from less than one to over 20
years (Appendix A, Tables A7 and A8).

The reports which teachers make are of two types: those dealing
with performance in a subject area and tutorial or pastoral reports.
Teachers were asked to indicate the numbers of each they would be
preparing for students in the various age groups in the current school
year. Table 4.4 illustrates the annual production of reports by teachers.

Table 4.4: Annual production of reports

Number of reports	Subject reports (N = 647) % teachers	Tutorial reports (N = 435)† % teachers
1 — 30	3	36
31 — 60	4	42
61 — 150	14	13
151 — 210	19	3
211 — 300	25	2
301 — 450	20	3
More than 451	15	1
Totals	100	100
Non-respondents	15	9

† Two hundred and twelve teachers did not produce tutorial reports.

It is clear that some teachers had a very heavy burden and nine teachers recorded very high involvement in the production of both subject and tutorial reports (i.e. they had an annual load in excess of 300 reports of each type). More typically, the annual production of subject reports was 300 or fewer, and few teachers wtih pastoral responsibilities were required to produce more than 60 tutorial reports.

In order to get some idea of the time commitment involved, teachers were asked to give details of the latest set of subject and tutorial reports completed, a 'set' being defined as comprising reports on pupils in a single year group. The number of reports in such 'sets' clearly varied. Just over a third of teachers preparing subject reports were doing so for 30 or fewer pupils, and only a quarter had over 90 such reports (or the equivalent of three classes of 30 pupils). However, a sizeable minority were preparing reports for the equivalent of more than five classes in the same year group at one time and most were also preparing reports for more than one year group (Table 4.5).

The time spent on a set of subject reports varied from two hours or less (34 per cent of teachers) to more than ten hours (ten per cent of teachers), the average being just under 5½ hours. The average time

Table 4.5: Number of year groups reported on at one time
(subject reports)†

Number of year groups	% teachers
1	38
2	23
3	13
4	14
5	10
6	1
7	1

† Forty per cent of schools did not contain all seven year groups of
the secondary age range.

spent on each report was just under six minutes. The age of the students appeared to have little effect on the time spent by teachers on
each report. A variation, however, was found between the different
report formats. Whilst report books and sheets took on average 4½ and
5 minutes respectively to complete, slip reports took nearly 6½ minutes.
Although most teachers recorded times close to these averages, a small
number took considerably longer or shorter in each case.

With so little time spent on the record of what in some cases represents a year's achievement it is not surprising that the results were
deprecated by many teachers. To do justice to the situation, it is necessary to point out that in many cases the 'writing time' is but the con-
clusion to a series of activities associated with assessment and recording
throughout the year.

Over 60 per cent of teachers also reported on the latest set of
tutorial reports completed, either in their role as form tutors or as
house or year heads. Only a quarter of teachers completed more than
30 pastoral reports; the majority, therefore, were reporting on the
equivalent of one class. The average time taken to prepare a set of
tutorial reports was 4½ hours but a substantial proportion of teachers
(17 per cent) had spent more than ten hours on the task. The average
time spent on each tutorial report was considerably longer than that
involved in the preparation of subject reports. The average time for

each report (all types combined) was just under ten minutes and, once again, the slip system was found to take rather more time to complete than either the report book or the single sheet.

In order to clarify the relationship between the number of reports prepared and the time spent on each one, the number of reports completed by teachers was cross-tabulated with the time spent in their preparation. The results for subject reports are shown in Table 4.6. A very highly statistically significant association emerged, with more teachers with a heavy reporting load spending on average less time per report than their colleagues on whom fewer reporting demands were made. Thirty-seven per cent of those with over 90 reports, for example, spent two minutes or less on completing each, as compared with only 11 per cent of teachers with 30 or fewer reports. Conversely, only eight per cent of the former group spent an average of eight minutes or more per report as compared with 38 per cent of the group with 30 or fewer reports.

The sample included 31 teachers in their probationary year and they were given a similar reporting load to their more experienced colleagues. But the average time they spent completing their subject reports during the spring term was almost three hours longer (i.e. eight hours and twelve minutes) than the average for the whole sample.

Table 4.6: Average time spent by teachers on subject reports according to the number completed†

Average time (mins)	Number of teachers completing:							
	1–30 reports		31–90 reports		91+ reports		Total	
	N	%	N	%	N	%	N	%
2 or less	25	(11)	37	(15)	61	(37)	123	(19)
3–4	48	(21)	94	(37)	54	(34)	196	(30)
5–7	71	(30)	82	(33)	34	(21)	187	(29)
8 or more	89	(38)	38	(15)	14	(8)	141	(22)
Total	233	(100)	251	(100)	163	(100)	647	(100)

† A chi-square test was applied to the data in this table and yielded the results $\chi^2 = 103.76$; $p < .00001$.

The preparation of reports

Sixty-four per cent of teachers used non-teaching ('free') time for subject report preparation although such opportunities were inevitably reduced by 'cover' for absent teachers, and teachers complained of 'constant interruptions' and the lack of a suitable work place in which to concentrate. Report books and single sheet reports were frequently held in the staff room and teachers were obliged to prepare reports there. Many teachers expressed their dislike of this practice. Eighty-six per cent of teachers completed their reports outside working hours and most expressed a preference for doing such work at home. The same pattern was repeated for tutorial reports although there was a tendency for rather more work to be done away from the classroom and the school.

Ten per cent of the teachers recorded preparing some of their subject reports during teaching time — a practice viewed as undesirable by some. In one school where the reporting timetable made this practice essential many of the teachers recorded their disapproval. The preparation of the report was often the culmination of a series of activities such as examination and marking, and most teachers were allowed only a short period of time (one or two weeks) in which to complete reports, which exacerbated many of their problems. To help in the completion of reports, a number commented on the value of keeping accurate and up-to-date records and some suggested the keeping of a collection of appropriate comments throughout the term, either using the regular 'mark book' or a note book to record examples of the pupils' classroom activity. Some also commended the adoption of various systems to highlight exceptional performance — good and bad — either by the use of symbols or pens of different colour.

Many teachers recorded their frustration with the repetitive tasks associated with 'heading up' a report, the completing of the student's name, subject, teacher's name and so on. Such details seem unavoidable although the slip system appears to magnify the number of clerical tasks. Another major task associated with that system and usually undertaken by the form tutor is the collation of the numerous slips provided by the subject teachers, the pastoral tutors and occasionally the head teacher. Also onerous in terms of the time involvement is the checking of reports written by other teachers. This is independent of the type of report in use and, as noted, earlier, is often carried out more than once, for example by both form and year or house head, with the head teacher carrying out the final check. Often associated with checking was the responsibility for finding the teacher whose report was unsatisfactory and ensuring that the error was rectified. Where the whole report required rewriting, as happens with the sheet or book system, the responsibility for the recirculation of the report was frequently handed over to the teacher giving rise to the problem. This was seen as providing an element of 'biblical justice'!

Summary and discussion

It is important to emphasize that in this chapter we have been concerned only with actual production of the report -- not with the assessment or record keeping activities which may precede it, nor with the discussions with pupils and parents which may follow it.

In examining the involvement of school staff, again the head's involvement in reporting was noted. Many heads themselves contribute reports on children they teach and while in ordinary schools the majority delegate responsibility for coordinating and supervising the reporting process, some two thirds are involved in checking the final product before it leaves the school premises. Such was the perceived place of the report in establishing and maintaining the image of the school, that several checks were commonly carried out to ensure its final quality. Heads were rarely involved, however, in scrutinizing parental replies — a task most commonly carried out by the form tutor.

Two thirds of the teachers sampled had 300 or fewer subject reports to complete each year, and those with pastoral responsibilities generally did not have more than 60 pastoral or tutorial reports to complete. The average time for completing a subject report was computed at just under 6 minutes, and a tutorial report at just under 10. This means that a teacher with, say, 300 subject reports (and only one third of teachers had more than this) would spend 28 and a half hours, or the equivalent of 43 school periods of 40 minutes, on reporting each year. Whether this is too long, too short or about right is difficult to judge. Just over five minutes to report on what may be a year's work for an individual pupil does not appear over-long. Writing the report, however, may be regarded as the tip of the iceberg, and is (or should be) underpinned by many hours of work in assessment and recording throughout the year. Another angle is to consider each pupil's report as a whole; if we take, for example, a first-year studying ten subjects, the total subject teacher time spent on his report would be 57 minutes, with a further ten minutes for the tutorial comment — 67 minutes in all.

One very clear and perhaps predictable finding was that the more reports teachers have, the less time they spend on each. The age of the pupils being reported on was not related to the amount of time teachers spent on their reports. The type of report, however, was, with report slips taking longer than single sheet or book reports.

A number of heads questioned whether the time taken to prepare reports might not more profitably be spent in other ways: 'Although it should not interfere with the basic duties of teaching, marking, preparation, etc. it clearly does so', reported one head, while others regretted that time did not always allow teachers to devote as much attention to reports as was desirable. The importance of staggering the reporting load for teachers throughout the academic year was stressed by some and one head noted an improvement in the quality of reports when their number was reduced and wrote: 'As with most things one is dependent on the staff who vary in their ability to be perspicacious, succinct and helpful. I find, however, that one report a year is generally more thoughtfully done than reports twice a year as we used to do . . .' A contrary view, however, was that termly reports were necessary to produce any real effect.

The common practice of crowding reporting into the few weeks after examinations, often at the end of term, clearly made difficulties more acute and again emphasizes questions concerning the timing of reporting — this time from the point of view of school organization — which were first raised in Chapter 3.

Chapter Five

Major Concerns in Reporting

After seventeen years report writing is still one of my most disliked tasks and only partly is this because of the work load. To some extent . . . it serves to emphasise how little one knows of some pupils in class situations but in all cases I find it rather disturbing to make rather sweeping statements about pupils whom one knows only in an academic classroom context. It seems likely that some pupils may be harmed by statements made in ignorance of all previous history, home background etc. even when one endeavours to make comments positive and constructive. The checking of colleagues' reports confirms my suspicions that in many/most cases teachers resort to the banal cliché or otherwise empty statement in order to avoid the problems . . .

(From a teacher's questionnaire.)

We move on now to examine some of the difficulties and concerns which heads and teachers identified as being associated with reporting and with the processes which lead up to it. The chapter begins by examing heads' and teachers' views of the pros and cons of different reporting systems and then goes on to look at wider issues relating to the production of reports of any type – the particular problems faced by teachers in different subjects; the demands of report writing for pupils of different abilities, for parents whose mother tongue is not English and, most important, problems relating to grading and assessment which underlie so many of the apprehensions concerning reporting expressed by heads, teachers and parents. The chapter concludes with a discussion of the preparation and training which teachers receive to help them meet the demands of reporting.

An appraisal of different systems

Problems associated with particular systems of reporting were cited relatively infrequently in comparison with those relating to more general issues.

Single sheets and report books appeared to produce the same problem of time wasted queuing for the report to be completed by another teacher. Both systems provided little room for comment, with, in the words of one head, 'little scope for staff who are perceptive, articulate and literate to provide a rounded in depth report'. Both were also open to the 'halo effect' where one teacher's remarks might influence subsequent comments. In the course of the project the team met a number of heads who said they had withdrawn individual reports of this type, recirculated them to teachers in a different sequence and obtained a quite different report as a result.

The slip system entailed organizational expertise and, as noted in the last chapter, a heavy clerical load on the staff who had to collect and collate the individual slips. Such reports no longer provided an overview of the students' achievements 'at a glance', and were seen by some head teachers to lead to a lack of continuity. Their bulky nature also led to problems of storage and some heads complained of the resulting proliferation of filing cabinets. A number also recorded that the extended comments which such reports demanded were an added burden to the teacher. One disillusioned head pointed out that 'the use of clichés remains — not so much the fault of the system as of those who use it'. Another recorded that 'some older staff need a great deal of encouragement to use the full reporting procedures', pointing out that a change of system may not necessarily bring about any change in behaviour on the part of the staff involved.

The slip system was found more commonly in schools where the system of reporting had been changed within the previous five years — an association which achieved a very high level of statistical significance, (Appendix A, Table A9). It should be noted that significantly more heads of schools where the slip system was in operation recorded supportive comments from teachers, compared with schools which used sheets or report books. Of equal, if not greater, importance was the finding that significantly more head teachers also recorded parental support for the reporting system where slip reports were in use.

Issues common to all reporting systems

Cost

As well as time, which was discussed in Chapter 4, cost was among the more commonly mentioned problems associated with reporting. Such problems, particularly where a reporting system is changed, are well illustrated in the following quotation:

> A critical issue within the school administration is the *cost* of the report system and its share in capitation allowance. There is no doubt that the revised system which we have adopted is going to prove expensive and will demand a far greater share of capitation than the report book system previously in use here. I feel that the increase is justifiable in terms of professional service improvements but teaching materials etc. are also a major priority and one is anxious not to reduce the money available in this way.

Professional printing costs, NCR paper, and the need to order in bulk to minimize unit cost were all mentioned as problems. A number of heads complained of the difficulties arising from a large stock of report books or sheets which had been rendered inappropriate by changes in the curriculum or in school organization, but which could not be jettisoned because of the apparent waste and the expense of introducing a new system.

The demands of different subjects

Almost one third of the teachers recorded some difficulty with grading or reporting in their main teaching subject with the proportion of teachers varying widely between subjects (Table A10). The subject areas identified as giving rise to the least difficulty were commerce (nine per cent), the sciences (14 per cent) and mathematics (15 per cent), whereas those proving most difficult were aesthetic and craft subjects (43 per cent), English (51 per cent) and remedial education, where almost three quarters of the specialist teachers recorded that they encountered difficulty. Heads were asked to indicate which subjects they considered inherently difficult to grade or assess and generally the proportions identifying such difficulty reflected the pattern found among subject teachers, although there were some differences. No head, for example, identified modern and classical languages as areas which might give rise to teacher difficulties in grading or assessment and the proportion of heads identifying problems in any subject area was usually much lower than that among the specialist teachers.

There was a large measure of agreement between teachers and heads of school concerning the nature of possible difficulties.

The major problems identified were:

(a) Subjectivity (especially in aesthetic and craft subjects, English and the humanities).

(b) Differential performance in different aspects of the subject (remedial education, English, aesthetic and craft subjects, modern languages, physical education and science).

(c) Achieving accuracy without demotivating low achieving pupils (remedial education, science, mathematics).

(d) Isolating what was to be assessed and reported upon (physical education, aesthetic and craft subjects and English).

(e) Attempting to report on pupils where limited contact meant that many pupils were unknown to the subject teacher (religious education, music).

Teachers attributed some of their problems to limitations imposed by the system of grading, particularly where very different standards of performance — for example in theory or practical work or in oral and written work — had to be subsumed within a single achievement grade. Despite the diverse nature of many mathematical activities, mathematics teachers did not identify this as a problem.

It had been thought likely that problems might arise more commonly where teachers were involved in teaching outside their main subject area. However, although almost a third of the teachers (199) taught and reported on subsidiary subjects the overall incidence of problems was somewhat lower (23 per cent) than with the main subjects. The nature of the difficulties remained unchanged although the problem of inadequate contact time was more frequently mentioned.

Reporting on classes with different ranges of ability

Teachers were asked whether the classes on which they had most recently reported contained (a) 'the full range of ability in the school',

(b) 'a wide range of ability but not all abilities' or (c) ' a limited range of ability'. They were then asked if the range of ability in the class had given rise to difficulties in reporting and, if so, what the nature of these was. Forty per cent of teachers had completed reports for classes containing the full range of ability, 29 per cent for classes with a wide ability range but not all abilities and 31 per cent had classes containing a limited range of ability. Only 13 per cent of the teachers altogether reported that the ability range within the classes had presented them with difficulties. Classes with 'a wide range of ability but not all abilities' seemed to give rise to least difficulty, with problems being recorded by seven per cent of teachers, whereas full ability and narrow ability classes gave rise to reporting problems for more teachers (14 per cent in each case).

Regardless of the ability range in the class the dominant problem was perceived as relating to students with low levels of achievement. Such students featured in more than half of the teachers' comments and the difficulty centred on the 'motivation' and 'encouragement' of low achieving students and the problems of providing 'positive' comments while retaining 'objectivity'. The remaining problems recorded by teachers were associated with the 'average' student, sometimes identified as 'the plodder', about whom teachers found it difficult to produce original or interesting comments.

Reporting to parents whose mother tongue is not English

A number of schools in the survey raised the problem of communicating with parents whose mother tongue was not English, but the only bilingual reports sent to the team were from Welsh schools. Although a number of Welsh schools provided reports only in Welsh, English was still the most common language used for reporting. In areas where Welsh was the language most commonly spoken in the home, bilingual formats, with terms in both languages, were commonly provided, the teacher's report being written either in Welsh or English.

The team visited a number of schools where the population included large proportions of children whose home language might be expected to be other than English and the parent survey involved one school with a large multiracial population. Here, members of a 'language support team' provided insight into the problems faced by those parents whose experience of written and spoken English was still limited. Some, whose use of spoken English was rudimentary, were fearful of attending parents' evenings; others whose command of written English was small had particular difficulty with the language used by many teachers on the report. The slip system of reporting, with its emphasis on lengthy verbal statements, was seen as particularly inhibitory. For many such parents a brief comment with a numerical grade appeared to lead to fewer problems. A commonly recorded experience was that parents were unable to understand that although the child was 'doing well' it was still possible to be entered only for CSE examinations. Clearly, problems such as this, which occur even where there are no language barriers, are likely to be more acute where a basic knowledge of English is lacking.

Although no examples of written reports in other languages were found, a number of schools provided oral translations at parents' evenings and this facility was welcomed by the parents. In other schools, however, students were expected to act as translators in any conversation with teachers, and concern was expressed by some teachers as to possible inaccuracies of translation.

Grading and assessment policies and practices

Many of the problems heads and teachers raised concerned grading and assessment. Ninety per cent of schools provided achievement or attainment grades on the report to parents and in the majority there was a school policy concerning the basis on which the grades were arrived at which applied to teachers in most subject areas.

In just over half (364) of these schools the same assessment policy was applied to all year groups and usually the dominant criteria were normative. (This meant that the attainment of an individual was related to the achievements of a larger group such as the other members of the class or the school year.) However, in 122 schools with an all-through assessment policy attempts were being made to combine two or more criteria for the creation of a single assessment grade on the report. The majority of school policies demanding such multiple criteria were attempting to combine incompatible ipsative (where attainment is compared to the student's previous work) and normative assessment models.

In 42 per cent of schools the school policy on assessment varied with the school year. The greater flexibility inherent in such a system allowed schools to move the basis of assessment from a normative one in the early years of secondary education to one related to expected examination performance (predictive) in the later years (years four to seven). Perhaps because of this flexibility, in this group only one quarter of the schools (52) produced descriptions of policies which demanded the use of multiple criteria. A school policy of ipsative assessment was very infrequent, being found in only six per cent of the schools with a consistent all-through assessment policy and never exceeding eight per cent in any year group in those schools where the assessment policy varied by year.

The commonest method of recording achievement was by means of a letter symbol on a five-point scale (A-E), used in 44 per cent of schools where achievement grades were found. A further 18 per cent used a five-point scale together with a percentage mark. Number scales from 1-5 were used to record achievement in 13 per cent of schools and in a further four per cent these were used with percentage marks. Altogether, a quarter of the schools used more than one symbol to record assessment of achievement, varying either over different year groups or on reports issued at different times of the year to the same year group.

Sixty-three per cent of schools (466) recorded an effort assessment on the report and again most had a common policy concerning the basis upon which such judgements were made for all year groups. Schools were fairly evenly divided between the different criteria which provided the basis of the policy, with 49 per cent assessing effort ipsatively (i.e. on the individual's previous performance) and 41 per cent using a normative basis (the performance of the class or year). Ten per cent of the schools with an all-through policy were attempting to apply both normative and ipsative models to their effort assessments.

Sixty schools varied the policy on effort assessments according to year. No general trend towards a normative model as the age of pupils increased was detected and in the sixth form especially, ipsative assessment was far more common. Again, instances were found of schools attempting to apply both ipsative and normative models to some year groups. Over two thirds of the schools with effort grades used a five-point letter scale and around a fifth employed a five-point number scale.

Of those teachers who had used achievement grades in the latest set of reports completed (see Chapter 4), 41 per cent had used a normative criterion, such as the work of the class or year group, 13 per cent had given predictive grades based on expected 'O' level and CSE results and 11 per cent based their assessment on the pupil's previous performance. As might be expected from heads' descriptions of school policy, many of the teachers (35 per cent) were using multiple criteria, some of which were clearly incompatible. An attempt to clarify what basis was being used in assessments provoked this response from one teacher: 'This question is impossible to answer. A student's work is graded on his/her own progress, progress compared with others, ultimate achievement compared with previous work and others' work as well as effort.'

The difficulties for the teacher resulting from such an attempt can be illustrated by looking at the case of a very able student (i.e. normatively at the very top of the highest assessment category) who dramatically underachieves. In relation to previous performance the student should be placed in the lowest assessment category; in relation to the normative base within the class achievement will still fall within the top or second category. How can this be resolved when a single grade has to be produced? Such problems indicate a possible source for the rejection of grading strongly expressed by a minority of teachers. Possible conflicts between normative and predictive grading are somewhat less dramatic because public examination results are normatively scored and the question here is more one of the difficulty of achieving a common grade on two normative bases and of teacher consistency and accuracy.

Both heads and teachers were forthcoming in comments critical of their present assessment practices and in identifying what they perceived as more general assessment problems. Heads highlighted here the impossibility 'of slotting all pupils into a simple grading system and making that system apply to all subjects'. Some complained that the reporting system was dominated by grading; others that the assessment system was 'too concerned with academic progress and too little concerned with students' personal development'. Almost as many, however, recorded their view of the fundamental impossibility of an accurate assessment of human personality' and reported the reservations that they felt about 'encapsulating a personality on paper'.

Misinterpretation of grading was a commonly cited difficulty:

> Whatever form of grading is used — and in spite of printed explanations accompanying each report — the gradings are invariably interpreted as competitive (order of merit) and absolute, regardless of level of ability of the pupil and regardless, almost, of the school's intentions.

Other heads gave specific examples of the kinds of misinterpretation they frequently encountered:

There is a strong tendency to regard 'C' as a poor grade in spite of the fact the five-point scale is printed on the report.

Some teachers wrote of their confusion:

I am extremely hazy about grading procedures. My head of department is well-up in this field so I tend to follow my leader.

However, where grades were not included on the reports, problems did not disappear:

The danger is that parents and pupils will not be able realistically to discover 'where the pupil stands' because of the lack of any grading system or order of comparison.

Other problems centred on variation in criteria between subjects and teachers, the widespread confusion concerning effort and attainment and the lack of objectivity in all systems of assessment. Teachers' comments included words and phrases such as 'illogical', 'arbitrary', 'crude' and 'lacking precision'. Teachers commonly reported problems when they were expected to produce a 'normal' spread of marks within one small class and when the full range of grades had to be applied to a series of classes each containing a relatively narrow range of ability. Some wrote of situations which engendered misunderstandings: 'a "B" in a low set is quite different from a "B" in a top set. We are encouraged not to stress the setting but this confuses the pupils . . .'. Heads, for their part, noted the unwillingness of staff to apply a full achievement rating scale and the tendency to overuse the median grades and underuse both high and low extremes.

There are a number of techniques available for improving the consistency of assessments between teachers, the most commonly attempted being the processes of standardization and moderation. Standardization takes the scores achieved by a number of students and adapts them to a normal pattern of distribution. It assumes that the student group contains representatives from the full performance range within the total population and that differential achievements occur within the sample with a frequency whcih approximates to a normal pattern of distribution. It is most usefully applied to scores achieved on a common test marked to a common pattern. Where scores are derived from different sources — i.e. different tests — or from more idiosyncratically scored material the technique has little purpose. Within the school it might suitably be adopted when a whole year group with an ability distribution corresponding to the normal curve is given a common examination which is subsequently marked from an identical marking frame.

Moderation is more suitably used when assessments are derived from different sources. It normally involves a group of teacher-markers in some cross-marking with the aim of arriving at a consensus about the relative merits of scores achieved on pieces of work. It results in the eventual placing of all the assessments involved upon a continuum.

Almost a quarter of the teachers surveyed who produced grades for school reports made use of both techniques, 17 per cent used standardization alone, 21 per cent moderation and nearly 40 per cent used neither process. Many teachers recorded the value they placed upon experience in arriving at accurate assessments, rejecting the 'fairly complicated statistical study' involved in 'the adjustment of grades'. Others pointed out that standardization was 'unsatisfactory' because the department was 'not clear on precisely what was being assessed'. A number of teachers drew attention to their isolated position, where they were the only teacher of their subject or the only teacher involved in the particular reporting cycle. Others indicated that all such procedures relied upon cooperation and this was not always forthcoming. In schools where heads had recorded that there was a school policy concerning the basis on which grades were allocated, and that such a policy included standardization of marks to a normal distribution, just over half the teachers reported that they were involved in standardization. A similar proportion of teachers were involved where school policy prescribed moderation.

A number of schools indicated that they had pursued an alternative strategy: that of identifying and clarifying differences in assessment needs in different subject areas. The emphasis in such instances was clearly on within-departmental consistency rather than on attempting to achieve common inter-departmental practice.

While many of the heads drew attention to the problems of grading, they were critical too of teachers' comments on the reports, describing them as 'too bland', 'cryptic', 'ritualistic', 'trite' and 'minimal'. Teachers concentrated their efforts on finding erudite, lengthy substitutes for the word 'satisfactory'. Some heads also recorded that comments were destructive rather than constructive, offered examples of poor spelling and carelessness and displayed weakness in the pastoral relationship.

The problem of the variable contribution made by staff was frequently identified with staff attitudes and the need for training in report writing.

A case study of assessment and reporting

In order to investigate some of the comments made by the heads and teachers more fully, a case study was conducted of reporting and assessment practice in one school.

A school with a slip system was chosen so that the maximum amount of written information provided by teachers could be examined. Since one aspect which the team wanted to explore was the accuracy with which teachers could 'predict' public examination performance it was necessary to work in a school in which the grades were linked with future public examinations. For this reason the collection of information was restricted to reports provided in years three, four and five. It was decided to select a school which was coeducational, to allow an exploration of possible report differences for boys and girls, and comprehensive, to provide examples of reports produced for students of different levels of ability. The final consideration was that close collaboration with the school administration and the teaching and pastoral staff was essential.

i. *The information collected*

As it was necessary to analyse the reports of the same group of pupils in their third, fourth and fifth year and to obtain public examination results, the whole year group who had completed their period of compulsory secondary education in the previous year (1978) was selected for study.

The subject grades on all reports remaining on file were recorded, together with such variables as the sex of the pupil and the sex of the teacher awarding the grade. In order to establish whether any variations in grading patterns were replicated with other pupils of the same age group, grades from a cross-section sample were also collected, with all report grades to the third and fourth year groups in the school in 1978 being added to the data (see Figure 5.1).

Figure 5.1:   *Case study: the reports from which grades and teacher comments were collected*

Year			Longitudinal sample
1976			Year 3

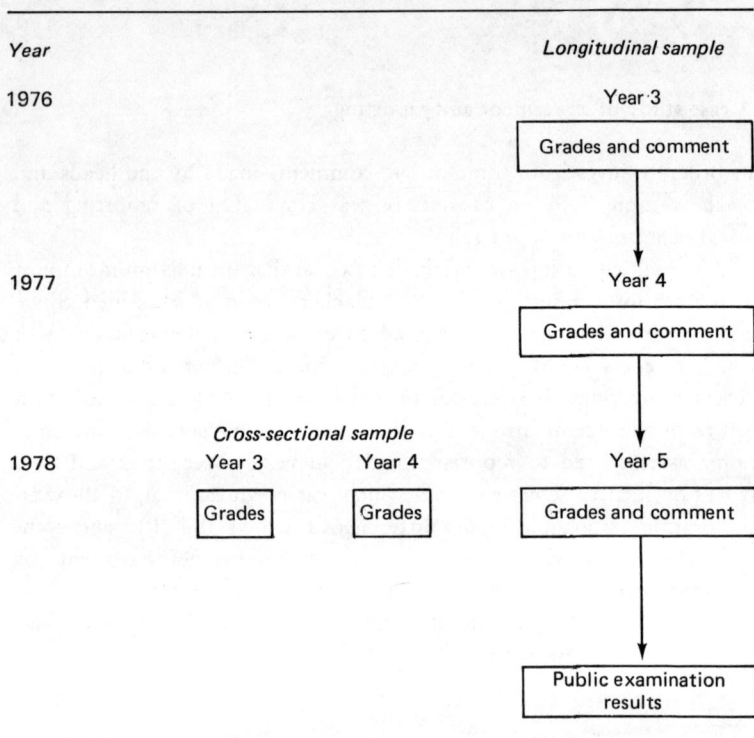

The grading system in the school was a six-point scale (A—F) although the use of four intermediate categories, A/B, B/C, C/D and D/E, extended the range in practice to a ten-point scale. Grades from year three onward were related to performance in public examinations but the term 'predictive' was rejected within the school as it was claimed that the grades indicated only the 'probability' of outcome. The following explanation appeared on the inside cover of the report:

Educational attainment: the level is assessed by estimated performance in public examinations:
A — Good 'O' level/possibly 'A' level.
B — 'O' level/CSE Grade 1.
C — CSE Grade 2/3.

D — CSE Grade 4.

E — CSE Grade 5/6.

F — Subjects studied but not presented in examination.

ii. The use of grades

Few schools appeared to have examined the distributions of the grades awarded to pupils and relatively little research has been carried out to explore the accuracy with which teachers can predict examination results (see here Murphy, 1979 and Postlethwaite and Denton, 1978). Many schools lay down fairly precise instructions concerning the allocation of grades and their predictive nature and it would not be a particularly onerous task to check how these are being applied, particularly where computing facilities are available.

Table 5.1 shows the distribution of grades over years three, four and five for pupils in the longitudinal and cross-sectional studies. Close similarities are apparent in the distribution of grades for the third,

Table 5.1: Case study: total grades obtained by year

(a) Longitudinal study

Grade	Grades allocated		
	Year 3 (N=2,010) %	Year 4 (N=1,331) %	Year 5† (N=1,021) %
A	3	3	2
(A/B	4	2	1)
B	15	14	11
(B/C	7	11	8)
C	26	28	22
(C/D	9	10	7)
D	22	18	17
(D/E	2	3	5)
E	12	10	20
F	1	2	7
Totals	101††	101††	100

(b) Cross-sectional study

Grade	Grades allocated		
	Year 3 (N=1,573) %	Year 4 (N=1,190) %	Year 5† (N=1,021) %
A	3	3	2
A/B	1	2	1
B	15	16	11
B/C	8	9	8
C	29	26	22
C/D	8	10	7
D	25	15	17
D/E	2	4	5
E	9	10	20
F	1	4	7
Totals	101††	99††	100

† Year 5 is common to both tables.
†† Rounding error.

fourth and fifth year of the cross-sectional and longitudinal samples, suggesting that the grading patterns found were characteristic of pupils at particular stages in this school, and were not idiosyncratic to a particular group progressing from the third to the fifth year.

The view, commonly expressed by teachers, that grading becomes progressively more severe, appears to be confirmed. Even in year five, however, teachers' grades were optimistic when compared with pupils' subsequent examination performance. Table 5.2 (which includes only those subjects where ten or more candidates were offered for examination) compares the grade awarded by the subject teacher in each year's report with the examination grade obtained. The table shows that in over half the subjects, the grades awarded to pupils were significantly higher in year five than the examination result. In no case did a teacher give grades significantly below those obtained in the subsequent examination. Hence, the claim made by some exponents of the 'labelling' theory, that teachers depress examination performance by 'harsh' grading, cannot be supported from this study.

Table 5.2: Case study: significance of difference between subject
teachers' grades and examination results†

Subject	Number of candidates	Year 3	Year 4	Year 5
Art	24	NS	NS	NS
Biology	78	††	$p<.001$	$p<.001$
Chemistry	16	††	$p<.01$	$p<.01$
Commerce	26	††	$p<.001$	$p<.001$
Drama	13	††	$p<.001$	$p<.01$
Embroidery	12	††	NS	$p=.001$
English	166	$p<.001$	$p<.001$	$p<.001$
Film studies	12	††	$p=.001$	$p<.001$
French	13	$p=.01$	$p<.001$	$p<.01$
Geography	77	$p<.01$	$p<.001$	NS
Geology	12	††	$p<.01$	NS
Housecraft	30	†††	$p<.001$	NS
History	50	$p<.001$	$p<.001$	NS
Mathematics	135	$p<.001$	$p<.001$	$p<.001$
Physics	24	††	$p<.001$	NS
Science	24	$p<.001$	$p<.001$	$p<.001$
Social studies	43	††	NS	NS
Spanish	27	$p<.01$	$p<.01$	NS
Technical studies	20	††	$p<.01$	$p<.01$
World religion	10	†††	NS	NS
Metalwork	10	$p<.01$	$p=.001$	$p=.001$
Technical drawing	50	††	$p<.001$	$p<.001$

† All significance levels indicate that the teacher grade was significantly higher than the examination result; NS indicates that differences did not reach .05 level of significance.
†† Subjects not included in year three curriculum.
††† Subjects with insufficient students for test.

Further analysis examined the allocation of grades to boys and girls by male and female teachers. Figure 5.2 shows the proportion of the different grade categories allocated by male and female teachers indicating that men tended to make rather greater use of the higher grades (A, B and C) whereas women produced higher proportions of lower grades (C/D, D, D/E and E). Although male and female teachers allocated a similar number of grades to the cohort in the period of the study, Figures 5.3 and 5.4 indicate that male teachers were teaching more boys and female teachers more girls. The different categories of grade were not awarded evenly to boys and girls as might have been expected, since both men and women awarded more of the higher grades to girls. Male teachers allocated a greater proportion of grades A, A/B, C and D and women teachers a greater proportion of grades A, A/B, B, B/C, C/D and D, to girls. Boys received a higher allocation of D/E and E grades from men and E and F grades from women. The greatest contrast was apparent near the bottom of the grade scale; here, ten per cent of the grades given to girls by both men and women teachers were E as compared with 15 per cent of those received by boys from male teachers and 23 per cent of those received from female teachers.

A number of hypotheses were offered by the teachers to account for this disparity of grade allocation between boys and girls – for example, that boys showed a greater tendency to misdirect their efforts. Some teachers ascribed the relatively poor showing of boys to local employment conditions where in 1978 boys were better assured of employment and thus less concerned about examination results, whereas girls had to compete for employment opportunities. Whatever the explanation, the superior performance of the girls was confirmed in the eventual examination outcomes. Figure 5.5 shows that the girls achieved considerably better results than did boys, being numerically dominant in the categories above CSE grade 4.

iii. Teachers' comments

Although teachers have frequently been accused of using a restricted and specialist 'code' when writing reports, little evidence in the case study was found to support this. Indeed many teachers wrote in an earthy everyday style which could hardly fail to convey the message. Most made full use of the space provided by the slip system although a few retreated to the 'satisfactory progress' model. Most reports gave the appearance of personal knowledge of the pupil and some displayed an almost vitriolic use of language:

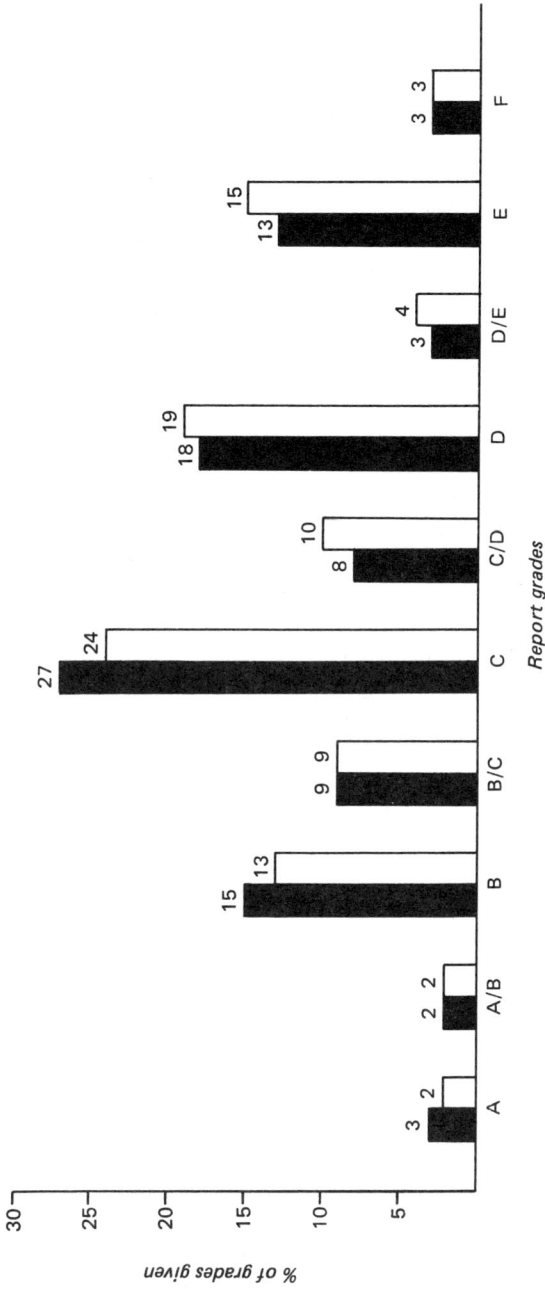

Figure 5.2: *Case study: report grades allocated by male and female teachers to years three, four and five (longitudinal sample)*

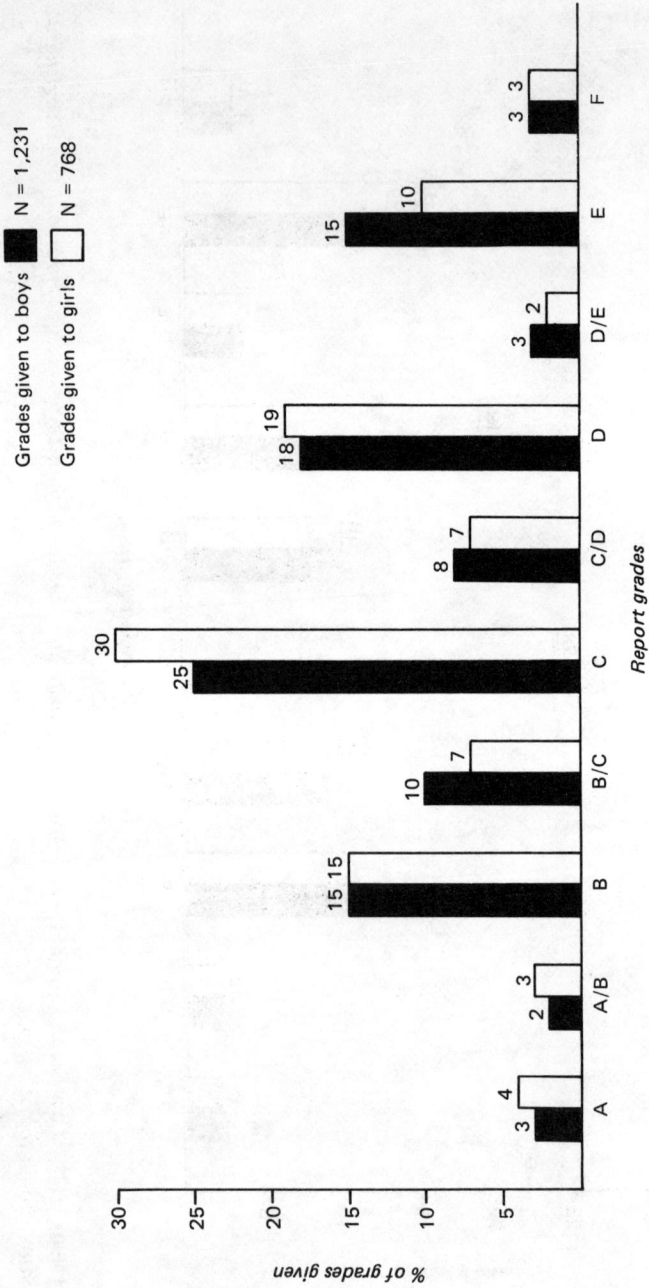

Figure 5.3:   *Case study: report grades allocated by male teachers to boys and girls in their third, fourth and fifth years (longitudinal sample)*

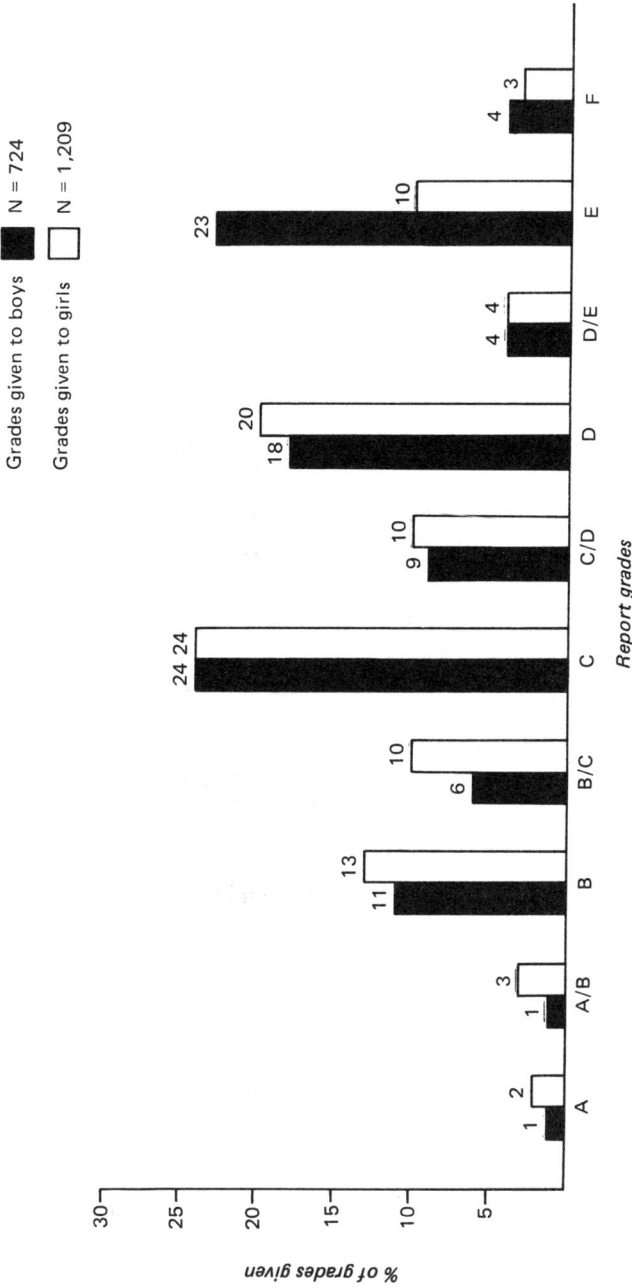

Figure 5.4: *Case study: report grades allocated by female teachers to boys and girls in their third, fourth and fifth years (longitudinal sample)*

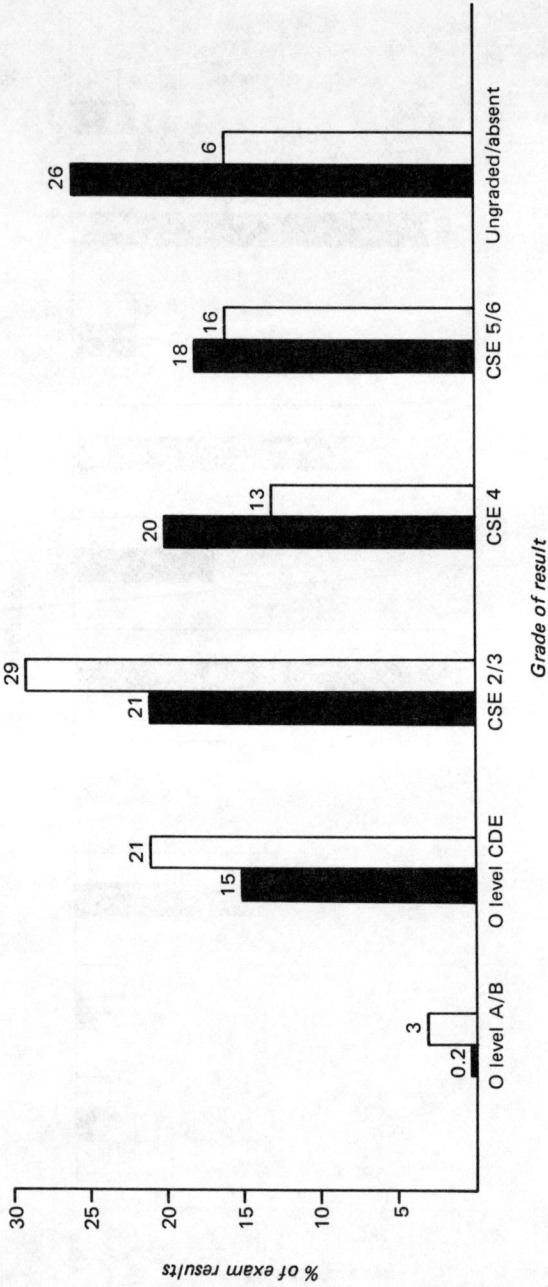

Figure 5.5: *Case study: examination results for boys and girls (1978)*

E— has been a constant disruption in the class. He has shown no interest in the lessons. He has arrived very late and without his books. If I gave him paper to write on, he still did nothing. He was noisy, often deliberately prevented others from working and his language was frequently unpleasant . . .

Such honesty was not uncommon and teachers certainly did not hide their classroom problems behind bland phrases. A year later the same student received this report in a different subject:

E— has not worked well this year. He has gone through months of misbehaviour, arriving late and with no books and disrupting lessons by agressive behaviour. As a result of his prolonged stupidity E— actually scored less than the class average although he is one of the brightest boys in the set . . .

However, the absence of influence from the views of others inherent in the slip system was amply illustrated for the same report contained the views of another teacher that:

E— has shown a remarkable improvement in his approach to the subject this year both in the classroom and with his homework. I hope that he will sustain this until the public examinations . . .

Such concerns were not untypical. The 'examinations' and the 'future' provided the orientation for much that was written throughout the three years for which reports were analysed.

Although examples could be found of the sarcastic, the superficial, the flippant and the downright petulant, many reports recorded positive achievements, although some could be seen to conform to what Winter (1976) called the 'diplomatic style': '. . . she has a generous heart. I am glad she is in my class.' Many of the reports, moreover, reflected the inconsistency of individual behaviour and showed that teachers did not subscribe to presenting simple 'black' and 'white' pictures of pupils:

. . . sometimes she is a model pupil and works hard and well. At other times she is very silly, playing jokes, arriving late and rushing round the classroom. I hope she will try to have more good days!

Occasionally it was not easy to comprehend meaning. One such example was where, beside a mark of 33½ out of 100, the teacher had written: 'Examination result is very exact but ought to be 60%.' Occasionally also where advice was given it was of a generalized nature and sometimes it was difficult to see how to act upon it: '. . . he should aim for neat and clear methods which show insight.' There was, too, some evidence of confusion between students in the same group, or of a set pattern of reporting — one teacher, for example, used identical phrasing on half the reports written.

The content of the reports was classified using a coding frame constructed from an analysis of a large sample of the schools' reports. This frame was divided into 13 areas concerned with teaching, one concerned with administrative matters such as attendance and uniform and one which included comments which were specifically pastoral.

The distribution of subject teachers' comments within these categories indicated that some aspects of the pupils' life within school formed a large proportion of the written content of reports in all three years (Table 5.3). Notable among these were comments concerned with effort and ability. Others, such as comments dealing with behaviour in class and the pupil's attitude to the subject, showed a small decline over the three years while a third group increased in the frequency of their use. In this last group were suggestions for remediation, comments on attendance and indications of possible performance in public examinations — although this last group still accounted for only 11 per cent of comments in year five. The proportion of the report content concerned with examination results reflected the incidence of third-year option-related school examinations and the 'mock' examinations preceding the public examinations in year five.

Suggestions from teachers, parents and students had directed the attention of the team to what was described as a 'negative bias' inherent in many school reports. In order to investigate this, teachers' comments were categorized according to the coding frame shown in Appendix A, Table A11 and were further classified as positive, negative, or 'moderated' — this latter classification being used to describe comments which mentioned both good and bad aspects of the student's performance or behaviour, or which indicated that the pupil possessed an attribute to a moderate or average extent. It was thus possible to get some indication of how positive or negative the reports in years three, four and five were (Table 5.4). Positive comments form the largest category in all three years. In year three, when option

Table 5.3: Case study: comments made by all subject teachers
in years three, four and five (longitudinal sample)

Area of comment†	Comments		
	Year 3 (N=1,759) %	Year 4 (N=1,212) %	Year 5 (N=1,194) %
Ability	14	14	14
Attendance	3	6	7
Attitude to subject	10	8	6
Behaviour	12	8	5
Confidence	1	1	1
Effort	23	21	20
Examination results obtained	9	0	9
Homework	0	3	3
Maturity	2	1	2
Participation	5	4	3
Presentation of written work	6	9	4
Progress	8	9	8
Prognostic: future performance	6	10	11
Remediation: suggestions for improvement	2	6	8
Totals	101††	100	101††

† The framework of comment areas appears in full in Appendix A, Table A11.
†† Rounding error.

choices had to be made and in year five when entry to public examinations was under consideration 'negative' comments appear rather more commonly. At these two points the need to report 'honestly' is maximized since external standards are ultimately available against which to measure accuracy. Only in year five does the proportion of negative comments come near to the proportion of positive statements.

The view, then, which emerges from this case study is that teachers are generally careful and encouraging in their comments and are frequently significantly over-optimistic in the grades they award in com-

Table 5.4: Case study: positive and negative comments on reports
in the third, fourth and fifth years

Value attributable to	*Comments*		
the teacher comment	Year 3	Year 4	Year 5
	(N=1,725)	(N=1,136)	(N=1,104)
	%	%	%
Positive; encouraging	45	55	41
Moderated	26	22	21
Negative; critical	28	23	37
Totals	99†	100	99†
Comments unclassified	34	76	90

† Rounding error.

parison with pupils' achievement in public examinations. It provides a
valuable counterbalance to some of the comments quoted earlier in
this chapter, and may inspire individual schools to carry out similar
analyses into their own practice.

Advice and training for schools and teachers

So far, this chapter has focused on the difficulties which confront
teachers in preparing reports for parents, and indeed in the wider area
of assessment. Clearly the kind of preparation which teachers receive
for this part of their work is of considerable importance and because of
this the teacher surveys included questions which explored the extent
to which initial and in-service training had addressed relevant issues.
The support available to teachers within their schools was also examined,
as was that available to schools from their LEAs.

Table 5.5 indicates that little work on reporting occurs at the stage
of initial training or through in-service training and that it is largely
left for schools to organize their own forms of support. Less than a
third of the teachers had received instruction in the supporting skills

of assessment and statistical techniques in initial training or through in-service courses. Teachers were asked to isolate features of their initial training which had proved of value, and included among their responses was the handling of tests and testing procedures, information on the variables which affect performance, as well, in the words of one teacher, as a 'healthy disrespect for the use of refined statistical techniques on non-random class groups'. Some wrote of the value gained in their initial training from workshops concerned with case conferences and confidentiality and aspects of relations with parents.

Table 5.5: Teacher training and reporting

Course components†	Teachers receiving instruction on reporting††		
	Initial training %	In-service training %	In-school instruction %
Marking and assessment	29	24	57
Statistics	29	—	—
Reporting to parents	9	14	46

†¡Teachers may attend more than one course.
†† N = 647.

Seventy-three per cent of the ordinary schools provided written guidance on reporting and assessment for teachers. In half the schools this took the form of special report information sheets, these being supplemented in 18 per cent of the schools with a teachers' handbook. A teachers' handbook was the sole source of written guidance in a further one third of the schools.

Examination of the report instruction sheets received by the project indicated that these concentrated chiefly upon routine administrative details — completion dates, the organizational procedures for collection and collation, etc. Many of the longer guides in teachers' handbooks also focused on these details although usually the advice was wider-ranging and occasionally very specific on a number of issues, such as the grading of effort and achievement, the nature of written comment, grammatical advice, legibility, neatness and spelling.

Advice on grading frequently included details of the distribution

required, either in terms of the proportions or the numbers to be expected in each class. The numbers and proportion provided illustrated a
range of interpretations of the normal curve of distribution, with a
'normal' distribution often being applied to all classes even where
these were selected by ability. Occasionally teachers were exhorted to
follow the approved distribution, one school concluding the instruction
by stating: 'it is important to follow these instructions even if you do
not understand them'! In a few schools positive advice on how to keep
records in such a way that report writing might be facilitated was
included.

Instructions on legibility were numerous, some guides ruling out
erasure and crossing out and insisting on the full rewriting of any
reports including an error. Grammatical corrections were similarly
emphasized, with proper sentence construction and the avoidance of
contractions such as 'can't' or 'shouldn't' being particularly specified.
A number of heads provided a list of their most-hated words and phrases
while others offered correct versions of words that were commonly
misspelled by teachers.

Instructions on what to write on the report were varied, with items
prohibited in one school being advocated in another. The most obvious
of these were references to poor discipline within the classroom. In
some schools teachers were told to make 'no remarks on ill-disciplined
behaviour . . . since this reflects on the teacher', in others they were
requested to comment on '. . . personal qualities including character
and pattern of behaviour . . . do not pull your punches!' The 'tone' of
the report was a subject frequently referred to, with common reference
being made to constructive, positive and encouraging remarks. Teachers
were reminded that 'the report is not a means of punishment' but, in
other schools, that 'a vague platitude will not be sufficient'. A very few
schools urged teachers to write their reports bearing in mind the objectives of the course. A considerable emphasis upon the correct name was
common, with the full forename being specified in many cases; several
schools instructed that the reports should always begin with the name.
Extracts illustrating the diversity of approaches which have been adopted,
from the documents provided by four schools, appear in Appendix B1.

In those schools which provided written guidance on reporting, a
third of the teachers did not refer to the guide for the reports they
completed in the year of the survey. It is, of course, possible that once
expertise has been built up within a particular system no further reference
to written guidance is necessary.

Most schools obviously supplemented written instructions with oral reminders in general staff and departmental meetings. Only half of the teachers working in schools where oral advice was part of school policy claimed to have received such advice concerning reports they had completed that year. It should be noted here that guidance may be given and not be perceived as such by teachers and it is also likely that schools avoid repeating advice year after year to all teachers and give it only to newcomers. Induction programmes for new and probationary teachers were organized in less than half the schools. Such courses commonly included information on the school policy concerning reporting as well as on assessment.

Fifty-two per cent of schools had carried out some form of school-based in-service programme in the five years previous to the survey and in a number of cases this had included topics associated with reporting. In one instance an in-service exercise had been devised where teachers took part in a workshop in which they explored the effect of the school report on its recipients through role-playing techniques. The workshop also focused on the rationale underlying the assessment requirements of different departments, guidance in test construction using examples from school practice, and expositions in simple language of terms such as *frequency, mean, standard deviation, standardization and moderation.* Such approaches were exceptional and help with skills closely associated with reporting was most usually obtained through teachers' experiences as examination markers or in moderation processes associated with public examinations. Many teachers commended both GCE and CSE examination boards as invaluable sources of information.

Heads were asked whether their LEA had offered any advice on reporting procedures within the last five years and also whether there was any adviser or inspector with a special interest in reporting. Seven per cent of schools claimed to have received LEA advice and six per cent of ordinary schools reported contact with a member of the LEA advisory staff who had indicated an interest in reports to parents. Table 5.6 presents the advisory interest in reporting and other selected areas as seen by the heads of ordinary and special schools in the survey. Subsequent inquires to the LEAs where schools had indicated an adviser with a special interest, or which had issued advice (14 LEAs in all) revealed that in none was school reporting to parents formally included in the brief of any officer. Two had established working parties of head teachers and authority officers to consider records of pupils' progress but the implications of these for reports to parents had not been considered.

Table 5.6: Head teacher's record of local authority advisers
with a special interest in reports

Area of special interest†	Ordinary schools (N=740) %	Special schools (N=97) %
Community relations	22	18
Student pastoral care	19	18
Home—school relations	11	17
School reports	6	11

† Schools may record an interested adviser in more than one category.

The project received a copy of a discussion paper prepared by the Surrey inspectorate, based on visits to secondary schools, sixth form colleges and technical colleges and on questionnaires completed by heads, prinicpals and a sample of parents. The paper looked, among other things, at the information made available to parents and governing bodies and presented a series of questions, including some focused on reports, designed to stimulate staff discussion. These are reproduced in Appendix B2.

Summary and discussion

Despite the difficulties which teachers recorded relating to reports, there was virtually total acceptance that they were essential. While there was certainly evidence that teachers questioned the effectiveness of reporting in its present forms, then, there was no questioning of the need for a formal means of informing parents of their children's progress.

A large part of this chapter has been concerned with problems relating to grading and assessment, that is, the problems which in fact precede the reporting process and which clearly have a wider context than that of the report to parents alone. We noted the widespread use on reports of achievement grades (found in nine out of ten schools) and of grades for effort (used in nearly two thirds of the school sample). Problems concerning the meaning of grades, confusion over grading criteria, and teachers' reservations concerning the tendency of grades to produce an overemphasis on academic success were recorded.

It was apparent from the case study that teachers were far from achieving accurate predictive grading. Although the grades they awarded became progressively more severe from the third to the fifth year, they were optimistic when compared with pupils' examination performance. In over half the subjects studied, grades awarded in year five were significantly higher than results in public examinations and in none were the teachers' grades significantly lower. Teachers' concern about the possibly demotivating effects of low grades emerged in their comments concerning the difficulties of reporting on less able pupils and the case-study findings bear the interpretation that predictive grading gives rise to considerable tension with the teacher only reluctantly and gradually moving towards awarding grades which come nearer to reflecting the realities of the examination system. The pressures coming from both pupils and parents for predictions of examination performance, which are discussed in Chapters 6 and 7, deserve mention here.

The case study drew attention to interesting sex differences within the grading process, with men making more use of higher grades than women and both men and women awarding a greater proportion of the higher grades to girls, who in fact achieved better results in public examinations. It is not intended that generalizations should be made from this one example; what is important is that schools are aware of the likelihood of such differences and take steps to monitor them and consider them when making interpretations of teachers' grades.

Problems of assessment and reporting appeared more common in some subject disciplines than in others. Commerce, science and mathematics, for instance, seemed to present the teacher with relatively few problems as compared with such subjects as English, aesthetic and craft subjects, and remedial education. The indication here is that where there is no readily identifiable 'right' or 'wrong' answer and where a variety of pupil responses is acceptable, problems of assessment may be particularly acute. Grading in such subjects may be perceived by some teachers as arbitrary and inappropriate and the descriptive comment a far more useful method of conveying information about pupil progress. Our analysis of comments in the case-study school provided examples of the detailed insights which teachers were able to record about the pupils they taught, and their generally positive and constructive content was noted.

The benefits and disadvantages of the different types of report system as perceived by the heads and teachers are by now fairly well rehearsed and require only the briefest summary. Single sheet reports together with report books share the problems of providing little space for comment, the possible risk of a 'halo' effect influencing teachers' comments and administrative difficulties associated with teachers having to await their turn to complete a set of reports. The slip system, to which many schools have been changing in the last five years, while giving more space for comment, has the difficulty that it is not easy to get an overview of a pupil's performance at a glance. Additionally, it too brings with it administrative problems associated with time-consuming collation and storage. It is apparent from this study that reporting can be an expensive affair; where large stocks of a particular type of report are accrued this represents an investment which cannot readily be dissipated.

Schools face the problems of reporting on their own; very little evidence was found at the time of this research of support from LEAs either through their advisory teams or through guidelines produced for schools. Teachers, moreover, were unlikely to have received any preparation either in pre- or in-service training for the task of reporting, or for the related activities of assessment. Schools, then, were thrown back on their own devices and three out of four of those in the survey provided written guidance for their teachers on reporting and assessment procedures. The quality of such guidance was, as might be expected, extremely variable, with the focus in some cases being on routine administrative details rather than on guidance concerning the allocation of grades or the kind of information which should be offered to parents.

Chapter Six

The Pupil's Perspective

Only one in ten heads reported that they had received comments from pupils concerning the schools' reporting procedures and very few indicated that the views of students had been sought through bodies such as school councils. Comments from heads indicated that in the majority of schools, pupils' views were largely unknown, and some heads enjoined the project to find out what they were.

This chapter is based mainly on the responses of 2,016 students in six schools. Details of the schools and their reporting procedures appear in Table A4. Most of the pupil responses relate to the report which pupils had received not more than one week before the questionnaires were administered (late spring to late summer term, 1980). In the following paragraphs pupils' perceptions of the usefulness of the report, the difficulties they encountered with it and their preferences are examined. The extent to which the report acts as a stimulus for discussion among students and with teachers and parents is explored, as are students' intentions to change their ways of working or behaving as a result of it. The chapter ends by examining issues associated with student self-assessment and includes a study of self-assessment in a sixth form college.

Students' views of the reports' usefulness

The six schools studied provided examples of single sheet reports, a report book and report slips. All made use of grades and all save one provided a key explaining the basis of grading. One school provided only grades derived from continuous assessment in most subjects. The other five differed considerably in the space allowed for subject teachers' comments. Five of the schools provided a tutor's report and four a parental reply slip.

Four schools had a policy which specified that students should be informed about the assessment procedures used, usually by the form tutor or by a senior member of staff such as a head of house. Ten per cent of the pupils in these schools still recorded problems with understanding the marks and grades on their report. However, the first-year pupils from the two schools which did not provide information concerning assessment indicated proportionately more problems with understanding the meaning of the marks and grades on their reports than did first-year pupils in other schools. In general, the incidence of problems declined in successive year groups. A point of considerable interest was that the pupils in one school where the basis of assessments varied from department to department reported no more problems of understanding than their peers in other schools.

Students were almost evenly divided between the views that most of the report was useful in providing information about their progress in school, or that only some of the report was useful. Very few students totally rejected the report as conveying no useful information. In all schools students showed a very significant decrease in satisfaction with the report as a source of useful information as they progressed through the school, although the proportion of students identifying the report as containing very little or no useful information never exceeded 12 per cent (Table 6.1). There appeared to be no major differences associated with the type of report the schools used. There was, however, a very significant association between the proportion of the report which was identified by students as useful and their level of satisfaction with their progress in school (Table 6.2).

The proportion of the report which students judged useful was highest among those most satisfied with their general progress. Nevertheless, over half of the 185 students who were not satisfied with their progress still recorded that most of the report which they had just received contained useful information. It does not therefore appear that dissatisfied students reject their report as a matter of course.

Subject teachers were identified as providing the most useful information by 81 per cent of students with only ten per cent considering that the most useful information was provided by the form tutor. This pattern was unaffected by the age of the student. In those schools where a house or year tutor and the head teacher or deputy head provided a report few students felt that this gave the most useful information.

The relative value of grades and comments was not quite so clear,

Table 6.1: The proportion of the report which was considered useful by students, shown by year†

Useful proportion of the report	Students in each school year††				
	Year 1 (N=463) %	Year 2 (N=446) %	Year 3 (N=408) %	Year 4 (N=341) %	Year 5 (N=350) %
Most	60	53	45	42	33
Some	38	44	50	52	55
Little or none	1	3	5	6	12
Totals	99†††	100	100	100	100

† A chi-square test was applied to the data in this table; a value of χ^2 of 99.4 was obtained, which for 8 degrees of freedom was significant at the .001 level.
†† N = 2,008; non-respondents: 8.
††† Rounding error.

Table 6.2: Students' perception of the usefulness of the report and their satisfaction with their general progress†

Useful proportion of the report	Students' satisfaction with progress††			
	Very satisfied (N=356) %	Satisfied in most respects (N=773) %	Satisfied in some respects (N=637) %	Not satisfied (N=185) %
Most	67	49	35	52
Some	29	47	59	37
Very little or none	4	4	6	10
Totals	100	100	100	99†††

† A chi-square test was applied to the data in this table; a value for χ^2 of 113.58 was obtained, which with 6 degrees of freedom was significant at the .001 level.
†† N = 1,951; non-respondents: 65.
††† Rounding error.

although the majority of students (58 per cent) felt that comments from subject teachers offered the most useful information. There were considerable differences between schools, some showing a marked increase in the importance attached to the grades provided by teachers, with a corresponding decline in the value attached to teachers' comments. In one school, however, teachers' comments appeared to be particularly valued, with 77 per cent of the fifth-year students indicating that they offered more useful guidance than did grades.

The majority of pupils expressed a preference for marks or grades which compared their work with their own previous performance (i.e. ipsative grading). Normative assessment based on the work of the class was preferred by 21 per cent and on the work of the year by the remaining 20 per cent of students. Although there were minor differences between student opinions in different year groups there were no discernible trends with increasing age. Student choices contrasted strongly with the practice in the schools, none of which had an ipsative assessment policy for any year group.

Thirty-five per cent of students felt that the reports provided by *all* their teachers were accurate and fair and very few — only one per cent — felt that *none* of their teachers provided them with such reports. No major differences were found among pupils in different year groups, nor did boys and girls differ in their perceptions of their reports' accuracy and fairness.

Pupils were asked if their last report had provided enough information on a number of selected topics; the results appear in Table 6.3.

The information contained in the report was considered adequate by 60 per cent or more of the pupils in four main areas concerning their ability, their progress, the system of grades used and the student as a person. In all schools there was a remarkably consistent pattern regarding these four areas, with pupils showing a slight but steady decline in their satisfaction with the amount of information provided as they progressed through the school.

In strong contrast with the areas already discussed, most students were dissatisfied with the information provided by their reports about possible public examination performance and about future career and further education chances. While satisfaction with the information concerning possible 'O' level and CSE performance did increase among older pupils, this trend being clear in all six schools, no clear pattern could be found for the item concerned with information about career prospects and chances in further education. In two schools the pattern

Table 6.3: Students' perceptions of the adequacy of information provided on selected topics in the report

	Ability %	*Student as a person* %	*Progress* %	*The grading system* %	*'O' level and CSE chances*† %	*Possible career/ FE*† %
% of pupils considering the information provided was:						
Too little	19	33	21	27	58	77
About right	80	60	77	71	39	22
Too much	1	8	2	2	3	1
Totals	100	101††	100	100	101††	100

† Items concerned with public examinations and career and further education chances were answered only by students in years three, four and five.
†† Rounding error.

was fairly stable across the third, fourth and fifth years, in two other schools there was an increase in satisfaction with the information provided and in the remaining two the proportion of students claiming that they were given too little information increased. In one school 97 per cent of the fifth-form students felt that they were provided with too little information about career and further education possibilities.

The general impression concerning the report as being relatively unimportant in providing information related to career and educational prospects was further confirmed by student responses to two further questions. They were asked first whether their school reports had been helpful with making examination or course choices and, second, whether they had been helpful in career or further education decisions.

While 64 per cent recorded the usefulness of the report in helping with course and option choices only 41 per cent had found them useful for career and further education decision purposes. In the school where most of the fifth-form students had complained of inadequate careers information, over 70 per cent of the fifth year recorded that their reports had been no help at all in this area.

Problems and preferences

Three problems constantly recurred in discussions with students;

teachers' handwriting, grades and marks, and the sort of language used on the report. Pupils were therefore asked specific questions on each of these issues, as well as being offered an opportunity to provide examples of other problems.

The replies showed that only ten per cent of the students considered they had difficulty in understanding the grades which were provided, but a quarter had problems with some of the words and phrases used by teachers and 61 per cent found difficulties with teachers' handwriting.

One hundred and nine pupils furnished examples of other problems. The most frequently expressed were those concerned with the non-specificity of comments. One student recorded that 'the comments . . . seem to have been taken from an over-used list and were not really comments about me'. In one school a working party of staff, student representatives and parents was grappling with the problem:

Male teacher:	'Many kids are ordinary, normal, middle of the road. I wouldn't expect to be distinguished in a crowd.'
Fifth-form girl 1:	'I think we all like to be seen as individuals. Now and then, anyway. (Laughter.) Otherwise you can lose your concept of self. If you are seen just as 4C, or whatever, your self concept is lost . . . you are not an individual, you are just one of "them".'
Fifth-form girl 2:	'That's important when you are a teenager . . . you do have a developing sense of identity.'
Female teacher:	'Anyone who sees the class for maybe two or three times a week must write individual comments. If they don't there is really something wrong with what they are doing. The problems are for those who see them for just a single period . . .'

Students also quoted examples of 'mistaken identity' and of reports provided for subjects they did not take, while others mentioned contradictions between grades and comments. In schools where single sheet reports were used, a number of students complained that this frequently gave rise to the same word or phrase being used by several teachers.

Pupils were asked if they thought anything else should be included on the report and also if their last report had contained information that they did not want their parents to see. A quarter offered examples of items that they would like included and these emphasized a more detailed approach, with information about areas of work undertaken in the period prior to the report and indication of how successful the student had been in these. Students also wanted more advice on how to achieve better results, on what subjects they should take further and on which careers they should consider.

The emphasis throughout was on the need for practical and personal advice rather than generalized comments and exhortations to 'work harder'. A small group of pupils wanted more said about their behaviour, character development and personality; how they got on with other members of the class and with their teachers; and their general 'attitude to the subject'. A further group complained of a dearth of comment in particular subject areas and on social and extra-curricular matters.

Only 14 per cent of students felt that there were items which should be excluded from the report. Most common of these were comments concerning behaviour. Almost without exception examples of bad behaviour were resented, as were those relating to poor test and examination preformance, lateness and truancy.

Discussing the report

Discussions with friends and teachers

For most students, getting their school report was an event of some significance. Nine out of ten had retained their previous report and many of these (62 per cent) compared the results on their present report with this. Over 80 per cent of students reported that they had discussed their report with others in their class, and with other friends of their own age and almost a third had talked about their report with friends of different age groups.

In contrast, over half the sample had not discussed their report with any teachers. Table 6.4 indicates that there were considerable school differences. The higher incidence of discussion with teachers at School A may be accounted for by the fact that this was the only school where the opportunity for discussion between students and teachers was built into the system (i.e. timetabled). But clearly other factors also determine the extent of such discussions; School B, for

Table 6.4: Students' discussions with teachers about their current
report (from students' questionnaires)

Report discussed	Students in each school† Percentage					
	A %	B %	C %	D %	E %	F %
With all teachers	6	2	2	1	0	0
With most teachers	20	12	2	3	3	2
With a few teachers	44	40	31	27	40	24
With no teachers	31	46	65	70	58	73
Totals	101††	100	100	101††	101††	99††

† N = 1,986; non-respondents: 30.
†† Rounding error.

example, made no such timetabled provision, but the incidence of
student—teacher discussions was again higher than in the remaining
four schools. In Schools A and B the incidence of staff—student discussions about reporting increased as the students got older; in the
remaining schools it appeared that such discussions were no more
likely to occur among students in years four and five than they were
in the first and second years.

In all schools girls were more likely to discuss their reports with
teachers than were boys. Students' satisfaction with their progress
in school was not found to be associated with the incidence of discussions with teachers.

Two areas of student—teacher discussion were explored with teachers.
The first concerned information-giving about the reporting procedures
in their schools and the second, the discussion of individual reports.
In three quarters of the schools it was school policy to inform pupils
about assessment and reporting procedures and this was usually done
by the form tutor, or by the form tutor and a member of the senior
staff. Responses to the teachers' questionnaire indicated that where
such a policy existed, 56 per cent of subject teachers and 65 per cent
of pastoral tutors had given students information in the year of the
survey. In their comments some teachers pointed out that pupils
rapidly get to know the system and become 'bored' and 'cynical' in

response to constant reminders about the reporting procedure. Other teachers said that such information-giving could be 'effective and appreciated' but that much depended on the style of delivery. Most commonly it appeared that teachers responded to individual questions as they arose within the classroom. A number of replies mentioned the difficulty of explaining very complex systems, such as those with variation between subjects and between students in different ability groups. Many teachers considered that students were ill-informed and a number planned to provide more information about the reporting system in future.

With reference to discussion of individual reports with students, Table 6.5 indicates the frequency with which these occurred. Forty-one per cent of the subject teachers and the pastoral tutors did not discuss reports with any of their students. Fewer than one in ten subject teachers had discussed the most recently issued report with all students, although the proportion among pastoral tutors was somewhat higher (17 per cent).

Table 6.5: Teachers' discussions with students about the most recently issued report

Reports discussed	Subject teachers (N = 640) %	Pastoral tutors (N = 435) %
With all students	8	17
With some students	51	42
Not discussed	41	41
Totals	100	100
Non-respondents	7	0

Teachers' views on student discussions showed a division between those who saw them as desirable and those rejecting them as irrelevant and possibly 'dangerous', particularly if discussion took place before reports were completed. Many of the teachers opposed to discussions regarded the report as a communication with parents and saw no reason to involve the student. A few placed responsibility for the lack of discussion firmly with the students, explaining that 'no one asked'.

A number of teachers saw the discussion of reports with all their students as clearly part of their tutorial responsibility, while others identified specific pupils — the 'anxious', the 'unsuccessful', the 'lazy' and those with 'frequent absence' — for discussion. A crucial factor for many teachers was the timing of the report cycle and teachers complained that the issue of reports at the end of the academic year did not allow time for student discussions. Tutorial periods afforded an opportunity for discussions of students' reports in some cases.

A more detailed analysis of the teachers' replies about discussions with the students indicated no significant differences between the various subject specialists, nor was the age of the pupils a significant factor. A highly significant relationship was, however, found between the frequency of discussions and the teachers' length of experience, with the more experienced teachers being more likely to hold discussions with their students.

Discussions with parents

All except eight per cent of pupils reported discussing their current report with parents or guardians. Where such discussion took place it tended to be brief (56 per cent) rather than detailed (44 per cent). About half the pupils reckoned that the time was spent about equally on 'good' and 'bad' comments, with some 20 per cent reporting that concentration had been mostly on the 'bad', and 18 per cent, mostly on the 'good'.

The report and changes in behaviour

Pupils were asked a series of questions to discover if they intended to change their work or behaviour patterns as a result of the report they had just received. First, they were asked: 'As a result of this report will you try to change the way you work or act (a) at home? (b) at school?' Table 6.6 suggests that the report is a powerful stimulus (at least in the days immediately following its issue) to the intention to change, with three quarters of students reporting that they would try to change in school and a sizeable proportion indicating an intention to change at home. Further questions explored the effects of 'good' and 'bad' reports and it emerged (Table 6.7) that the majority of

Table 6.6: Students' intentions to change following the
current report

Work and behaviour	Students	
	At school (N = 1,698) %	At home (N = 1,914) %
Will attempt to change	76	42
Will not attempt to change	24	58
Totals	100	100
Non-respondents	318	102

Table 6.7: Students' resolutions following 'good' and 'bad' reports

Student resolution	Students†	
	After 'good' report††† %	After 'bad' report††† %
Will work harder	68	83
Will not change	30	8
Will work less hard or give up	3	9
Totals	101††	100

† N = 1,971; non-respondents: 45.
†† Rounding error.
††† A sign test was carried out on matched cases and a value of
z = 9.58 was obtained, significant at $\rho < .001$.

students claimed that after both 'good' and 'bad' reports they felt
like working harder, although the latter were clearly more effective
in producing such immediate worthy resolutions. It should also be
noted that the proportion claiming that they would work less hard
or give up was greater after a bad report. Girls tended to respond
positively — i.e. say they would work harder — after receiving either

a good or bad report, although differences between the sexes were slight. No associations were found between the pupils' perceptions concerning the fairness and accuracy of the report and intentions to change behaviour, or between pupils' satisfaction with their general progress and intentions to change.

Such marked reactions to both good and bad reports on the part of the students contrasted strongly with teacher expectations of the generally minimal effect of reports on students. A few teachers considered that reports maintained the motivation of successful students. Poorly motivated students, however, remained unaffected or were briefly affected at the time of issue. One teacher pointed out that reports were of little value since students 'are or should be aware of their position and level of effort' and a number deemed it unrealistic to expect the summary of a student's achievements over a fairly lengthy period expressed in a few words, to have much effect at all. Many teachers associated any positive motivational effects the report might have with the parents' reaction to it and instances were cited of pupils' pride in a good report being shattered by parents' indifference.

Student self-assessment: a case study

Ideas that students should be active participants in their own assessment are relatively new. During the early stages of the project contact was established with a number of schools which were attempting to improve the motivation of students by providing them with opportunities to take part in the process of assessment, but head teachers' replies from the national survey showed that self-assessment was very rarely used. In only two per cent of the schools did a student self-assessment contribute to the reporting process and, again, in only two per cent was the self-assessment an integral part of the report finally received by parents.

The most common use of self-assessment techniques was in the field of careers education (41 per cent of schools), where it was frequently used as part of the training in self-awareness. It was much less frequently used in other areas of teaching and, where it did occur, it was chiefly as a component of various courses in personal and life skills; its use was also recorded in community education, social studies and English (the SRA reading scheme includes self-monitoring exercises) and it also appeared in individual counselling schemes and in the preparation of leaving profiles for non-examination candidates.

Heads considered teachers to be the prime audience for information gathered via student self-assessment although pupils were almost as commonly identified as benefiting from the exercise, and just over a quarter of the head teachers thought such information might be of value to the parents.

Because the possible value of student self-assessment was quite widely accepted yet very few schools were actually using it, it was decided to conduct a case study to explore the working of such a system. Many head teachers had indicated that while they accepted the principle of self-assessment they had reservations about its application in the early years of the secondary school. It was therefore decided to carry out a case study of students aged 16 to 18 in order to obtain a picture of a system which would offer fewer problems of feasibility for most heads.

The 253 students concerned were attending a large sixth form college which, while not having an 'open access' policy, recruited a large group of non-traditional one-year students in addition to the academic 'A' level candidates. In the first year students completed two self-reports and those following a traditional 'A' level course produced a third self-report in the second year. These were sent to parents together with a series of subject and pastoral slips of a conventional kind.

It was seen as essential to obtain the views of staff, students and parents in order to build up a balanced picture of the system in operation. A semi-structured interview was carried out with the principal and with a sample of both subject and pastoral staff. Parents attending a parents' evening were also interviewed and group discussions were held with students (an opportunity sample of those not receiving formal instruction during each teaching period through the day).

The content of all student self-reports produced during the previous two academic years was analysed, with comments being classified into categories relating to areas such as progress, confidence, attitude and expectation of success.

In their self-report students were asked to provide information under the following headings:

Internal: ⎫
External: ⎭ list your active interests in and out of college.

Academic: assess your work, progress, response to courses; indicate problems.

General: mention any general problems; comment as you wish on yourself, your circumstances, the college.

Future: up-date your ideas, applications, etc.

Although many tutors obviously expanded upon this information and offered detailed guidelines for their students, a number did not and some student comments suggested that clearer instructions and explanations would have helped to bring about greater participation and a more thoughtful response. As it was, among traditional sixth formers, girls made on average four comments on their self-report, and boys, three. Among the one-year sixth formers, the boys tended to produce more comments than the girls. The largest group of comments, accounting for about a third of those made, was concerned with progress and most students wrote of progress in terms of specific difficulties which they had encountered. Student comment on examination performance was similarly problem-oriented. Despite the expectation by teachers that self-reports would reveal personal and home-based problems as well as difficulties with work, these were relatively unrepresented in the sample. Few students made use of their self-report to launch an attack upon their teachers or indeed to attribute to others responsibility for their particular difficulties or failings.

From the group discussions it was apparent that while students were clearly aware of the mechanics of the self-report system there was considerable confusion concerning the purpose of the self-report and some concern regarding the potential dangers involved in such disclosures. Many students, for example, were uncertain about who might have access to their self-reports and some were inhibited because of their anxiety that teachers in subject areas where they were encountering difficulty might see their comments. Other students were reluctant to be totally honest about their level of effort, as this was then seen by parents. Another group reported that they tended to minimize or disregard problems altogether since they feared that such disclosures could be damaging to their further education or career chances and they were concerned that their self-reports were used during the preparation of both the UCCA forms and references for potential employers. Some students felt it similarly unwise to produce critical comments either of teachers or of the college in general since it was felt that these too might provoke an adverse reaction. One or two who had felt strongly about aspects of college life or about particular teachers had had to rewrite their criticisms in more diplomatic terms.

In general, however, students did not consider the self-report an appropriate place to record their dissatisfaction.

Many students felt under no obligation to be particularly truthful concerning their interests outside college, as they felt that this section of the self-report intruded into their private lives and they tended to provide only what they felt the college 'wanted to hear'. Indeed, sometimes the information provided was so far from the truth that they were not prepared to show the self-report to their friends!

Students found it difficult to assess their progress with any degree of accuracy, as they felt that they lacked sufficient information about either the requirements of the course or about their own accomplishments. A number explained that they tended to reflect the grades awarded by teachers to 'get round the problem'. While students felt that the self-report provided an opportunity for the shy to seek help with problems, few attached much importance to the exercise and the advice they received from their tutors appeared extremely variable. Most students gave little thought to the content of the self-report, although a very small fraction of the students said that completing the report led them to analyse their progress and attempt to improve their own performance.

The principal of the college was an enthusiastic advocate of the student self-report system, feeling that, because the student's stay in college was usually limited to two years, it was vital to improve upon the information available from the conventional report. Knowledge of the students' reactions to their courses was seen as of great importance and the only 'constraint' placed upon students was that their comments should be courteous.

Despite considerable efforts on the part of the principal and senior pastoral tutors to involve and inform all the staff, there was confusion on the part of many of the staff about both the working and purpose of the self-report. Staff fears concerning the report were centred upon their belief that the students would tend to tell them what they wanted to hear. Discussions with staff confirmed the students' comments concerning the varied nature of the advice offered about the completion of the self-report, with some teachers offering careful guidelines and others insisting only upon speed.

Parents appeared unaware of the possible purpose of the self-report, most rejecting it as irrelevant, since they 'knew their own children' and the 'staff ought to know them'. Most also felt that the report could be of little value for the student and took a somewhat cynical view of its likely truthfulness. A small minority saw potential dangers for the student in such a record and feared that it might in time form a part of a certification process 'just like "O" level'. Such parents considered that it was a safeguard if the self-reports were seen by parents.

It is important to emphasize that general conclusions should not be drawn from this one example of self-reporting. In this case the college was eager to maximize the information made available about students during their short stay. In other schools the emphasis was on the possible improvement in the pupil's motivation which might result from a deeper understanding of his or her own performance. Such schools frequently retained the resultant self-assessment within the school and did not make it available to parents and it was claimed that student opinion supported this confidentiality.

One 13-to-18 high school which had used such methods for some years supported their use as follows:

1. It encourages students to feel that they have an important part to play in monitoring their progress and that what they have to say is valued.
2. They are participators in their own development and not just receivers of information.
3. It reinforces one of the college ideals, valuing the individual.
4. It forms the basis of a continuing dialogue between student and teacher.
5. It is a means of drawing attention to problems. Experience suggests that some students initially find it easier to write about a difficulty than to tackle the teacher in conversation.
6. It encourages students to look at themselves in a constructive way. This again is part of a wider ideal of the college, in that we hope we are encouraging students to know themselves better.
7. The writing of self-assessments implies values such as trust and honesty between teacher and student. These again are ideals we would wish to foster.

These are indeed powerful arguments for such a system of reporting, and difficulties of achieving the hoped-for outcomes in practice should not detract from their desirability. It is quite likely that the skills required to complete a self-assessment need to be developed over time and that, in order to avoid misunderstanding, the purpose of the exercise needs very clear explanation. Examples of the instructions provided for pupils were in other schools more detailed than those found in the case study reported here, as for example are the following from a 13—18 high school:

> How do you think you have been getting on since you wrote your last report (or, if this is your first report, since you started the course)? You might consider what you have gained from the course so far; the contribution you feel you have made towards the course; the effort you have put into written work, discussion, drama, practical work (this will depend on subject). Do you think you could put more into the work, and if so in which areas?
>
> Which parts of the work have you found difficult?
>
> Have you any suggestions as to how the course could be improved?

Another approach, this time in a sixth form college, was to ask a series of more sharply focused questions:

> Can I cope with the work? (i.e. the concepts and ideas rather than with the quantity demanded.)
>
> Is the pace too fast/too slow/about right for me in a given subject?
>
> Do I work hard — or too hard — or not hard enough?
>
> Do I let work pile up and frighten me, or am I learning to organise my own time?
>
> Do I like/need guidance, or can I get on better when left alone?
>
> Am I becoming more, or less, dependent on my teachers?
>
> Am I learning to use the library and/or other resources?
>
> Do I enjoy/tolerate/dislike the work in given subjects?
>
> Could staff help me more? (how? positive suggestions, please.)

Am I gaining confidence in my own ability?

Can I cope with the differing demands made on me by (say) tutorials, lectures and practical work?

What help would I most value during my next two terms at the college?

Self-assessment of this type may, however, also provide little information of value unless students and staff alike are aware of its aims and convinced of its likely benefits.

Summary and discussion

This chapter has produced several encouraging findings. First, most pupils were able to report that they understood the marks and grades on the reports they received and indeed in three out of four schools in the survey it was policy that students should be informed of the assessment and reporting procedures in use. It was noted that this was not always the simple task it might at first sight appear, but it does seem to be one that is worth the effort. In the two case-study schools where no such information was given, a higher proportion of first-year pupils experienced problems. Generally, students seemed to grasp the system fairly quickly and problems of understanding marking and grading systems declined in successive year groups. Other problems of understanding arose in connection with teachers' handwriting (reported by some 60 per cent of pupils) and the words and phrases they used (25 per cent).

Second, very few students rejected the report as conveying no useful information. The schools studied presented different types of reporting systems including examples of slips, single sheets and books, but there were no indications that students in any one system perceived it as more useful than those in another. Students' perceptions of the reports' usefulness tended to decline among older students and were also found to be associated with the students' general satisfaction with their progress. Subject teachers were seen as purveying the most useful information, with only one in ten students considering the most useful information came from their tutorial report. This may reflect the degree to which students appear to value comments which are detailed and specific. The non-specific nature of comments was cited as giving rise to problems and students made a plea for both detailed comment on work recently completed and detailed advice. It was noted in the study conducted on self-assessment that students' own comments on their progress tended to focus on specific aspects of their work, rather than on general description.

The majority of students, however, recorded that the information they received on their ability, progress and on themselves 'as a person' was adequate. The greatest discrepancies between what was desired and what was provided were found in relation to information concerning their chances in public examinations and their future education and career possibilities, where 58 and 77 per cent of students respectively recorded receiving too little information. While the report was found to be useful in helping with course and option decisions, the majority of students had not found that it had helped in decisions about further education or careers.

The third encouraging finding to emerge from this chapter is that, in the short term at least, the report stimulated the intention to change behaviour. Both 'good' and 'bad' reports were effective in producing a resolution to work harder, with bad reports the seemingly stronger stimulus (but with the danger also of inducing despair). It should, however, be emphasized that teachers were generally dismissive of the importance of such effects, believing that they were usually short-lived, and largely confined to reinforcing the resolve of the already studious. Any positive motivational effects that occurred were likely to be the product of the parents' reaction to the report, rather than the child's reaction to the information it contained.

While all but a few children reported having discussed their report with their parents, such discussions were reported by over half the pupils studied to be brief. There might be much to be gained if both parents and teachers recognized the possibilities of first, accepting children's resolutions to change at face value and, second, helping them to sustain their impetus and bring them to practical effect. For the teachers' part, it is unlikely that this could be achieved unless opportunities are found to discuss reports with students. Over half the students reported that they had not discussed their report with any of their teachers and just over 40 per cent of teachers had not discussed reports with any of their students. As might be expected, we found indication that the provision of time for discussion of the report helps the situation, but other factors too may be pertinent.

For example, the fact that more experienced teachers were more likely to hold discussions with students about their report may reflect the fact that some of these teachers have time allocated for pastoral or administrative duties, but may also indicate that they have acquired the degree of confidence and the skills required for a task which may need delicate handling. As noted in the opening chapter, while much has been written on assessment, little is available to guide the teacher in the art of mediating assessments. And so we have the somewhat bizarre situation that students discuss their report widely with their friends, almost universally with their parents or guardians, but in many cases not at all with their teachers.

Chapter Seven

Parents: Audience or Participants?

It was noted in Chapter 2 that the report was seen as having a variety of functions and in the last chapter its possibilities as a means of motivating pupils were discussed. The report's main function, however, is widely seen as being to convey information to parents concerning the progress of their children, and we saw in Chapter 2 how parents might be viewed simply as an audience for this information, or less commonly, how the report might be seen as part of a wider strategy of involving parents more fully in their children's education. In the paragraphs which follow, parents' views of the usefulness of the information they receive are explored, and, following the format adopted in the last chapter for the pupils, attention is focused on the difficulties parents encounter with reports and their preferences. The extent to which parents recorded talking about the report with their children is examined and contacts with teachers at parents' evenings are discussed. The chapter concludes by looking at the use made of that other common means schools offer parents for expressing their opinions: the parental reply slip. The data in many instances are derived from the questionnaire responses of 1,375 parents, whose children provided much of the information in the previous chapter.

Parents' views of the information provided by the report

The majority of parents who returned questionnaires thought that the report which they had just received contained 'some new information' on their child's progress and that most of the report was useful. Almost a third, however, indicated that it contained 'no new information' and seven per cent that the report was of very little or no use. There was a highly significant decline in the proportion of new information attributed to the report by parents of children in successive year groups (Table 7.1).

Sixty-five per cent of the parents felt that the most valuable part of the report was the teachers' comments, while the remaining 35 per cent valued marks and grades most. No significant trend could be detected in the relative value placed by parents upon teachers' comments as compared with marks and grades as their children approached public examinations, even though a number of head teachers and a vocal minority of parents had expressed the view that parents gave increasing weight to marks and grades at this stage. Three quarters of the parents saw the subject teachers as the most useful source of information and their views were remarkably consistent in all six schools. The head was not considered to be an important source of information in those schools where a head's report was included and few parents indicated that they wanted a head's report where one was not provided. In School F, which provided a form tutor slip, a sizeable minority of parents (32 per cent) indicated that they considered the form tutor to be the most useful source of information. In the remaining schools the proportion of parents nominating the form tutor as the most valued source of information varied between five and 15 per cent.

Parents were rather more satisfied with the fairness and accuracy of the report than were their children, with 85 per cent considering

Table 7.1: The provision of new information by the report in succeeding year groups — parents' views†,††

Amount of new information	% of parents with children in				
	Year 1	Year 2	Year 3	Year 4	Year 5
Much new information	20	11	10	7	6
Some new information	52	62	63	56	49
No new information	28	27	28	36	45
Totals	100	100	101†††	99†††	100

† A chi-square test applied to these data yielded a χ^2 value of 56.51, which with 8 degrees of freedom, is significant at the .001 level.

†† N = 1,375; non-respondents: 37.

††† Rounding errors.

that the last report had provided a fair and accurate picture of the progress made by their child. However, over half considered that the report did not provide a complete picture of their child's progress and a further 13 per cent were uncertain on this point. On none of the topics shown in Table 7.2 did parents consider that they had excessive information and while most were satisfied with the information given about their child's ability, progress in individual subjects and their child as a person, more than half felt that they were inadequately informed about their child's chances in public examinations, what the child was expected to learn in the various subjects, the nature of the teaching group in which that learning was supposed to take place and, most marked of all, the child's future choice of career or prospect of further education.

Parents thus agreed with their children in many respects about the adequacy of information provided on various topics, with the most pronounced agreement occurring over shortage of information about

Table 7.2: Parents' views on information provided by the report on selected topics†

	Ability %	The child as a person %	Progress %	What the child learns %	The teaching group %	'O' level/ CSE chances†† %	Career/ FE chances†† %
% of parents considering the information about their child was:							
Inadequate	27	28	19	56	61	53	79
About right	73	71	81	44	39	47	21
Excessive	0	1	0	0	0	0	0
Totals	100	100	100	100	100	100	100
Non-respondents	81	155	121	149	176	63	78

† N = 1,375.
†† Items concerned with public examinations and career and further education chances were answered only by parents with children in years three, four and five. The total sample for such items was 715.

public examination and career prospects. While the proportion of parents recording that they were provided with inadequate information about their child's prospects in the public examinations decreased with each year in all the six schools, dissatisfaction with the information about career prospects decreased in only two (D and F), and in one school, School A, the proportion of parents dissatisfied with the amount of information provided by the report actually increased in each of these last three years. It did not appear that the increasing level of parental anxiety could be accounted for by local employment factors peculiar to School A's situation.

Problems and preferences

As with the pupils, difficulties in reading teachers' handwriting were among those most commonly reported by parents. A similar proportion of parents (almost one third) were unhappy with the amount of information provided by the schools about the system of grading used on the reports, and 18 per cent reported difficulty in understanding the marks and grades used. It was found that a third of the parents recorded that they did not in fact know the basis upon which the grades on their child's report were determined and it seems therefore that the schools' attempts to inform them on this point had met with limited success. There was little variation in this proportion between schools, and parents' reported ignorance of grading procedures was not associated with any particular grading policy, or indeed the use of several grading policies in a school. Examples of the information on reporting and assessment given to parents in other schools appear in Appendix B3.

Forty-seven per cent of parents wanted the basis for assessment to be the pupil's own previous work (i.e. ipsative assessment) while 34 per cent thought the basis should be the work of others in the year group and 19 per cent, the work of others in the same class (i.e. normative assessment). The preference for ipsative assessment expressed by just under half the parents echoes the findings reported for pupils in Chapter 6. When parents' responses were 'matched' with those of their children, however, considerable divergence of opinion was apparent (Table 7.3). A common preference for ipsative assessment was found among only 31 per cent of the sample and even when all types of assessment are included parents and children agreed as to the assessment

Table 7.3: A comparison of parent and pupil preferences concerning the basis of grading

Pupil preference	Parent preference			
	Ipsative	Class normative	Year normative	Total
Own previous work (ipsative)	379	107	199	685
Work of others in class (class normative)	92	65	114	271
Work of others in year (year normative)	86	48	120	254
Totals	557	220	433	1,210†

† N = 1,375; 'unmatched' cases: 165.

basis they would prefer in only 47 per cent of cases. Differences between parents and children in the value given to teachers' comments as compared with marks and grades were also examined, and it was found that while 42 per cent of the parent–pupil sample shared a common view of the greater usefulness of teachers' comments and 18 per cent agreed in their preference for marks and grades, the remaining 40 per cent of parents and children held opposing preferences (Table 7.4).

Other difficulties concerning grading and assessment mentioned by parents included inconsistencies between grades and comments,

Table 7.4: A comparison of parent and pupil views on whether teachers' comments or marks/grades were most useful

Pupil preferences	Parent preferences		Totals
	Teacher comments	Marks/ grades	
Teacher comments	502	222	724
Marks/grades	246	216	462
Totals	748	438	1,186†

† N = 1,375; 'unmatched' cases: 189.

and problems in interpreting what a score meant because no upper or lower limits were indicated; a small group of parents made a plea for standardized scores. A few head teachers recorded that some parents 'rather simplistically' required orders of merit and marks such as they had received on their own reports. In discussions with parents, members of the team were often asked to explain why parents could not be provided with the percentage marks and class positions which they had, as children, received. Justifications which relied on the changing nature of schools, their educational rather than selective emphasis, and teachers' disillusion with the failures of the past were not always well received — although one father, who had systematically been provided with reports offering marks of between 18 and 40 per cent and class positions at the bottom of his class conceded that these had proved to be less than accurate predictors of his subsequent university career!

Commonly, parents made a plea for a more detailed and personal description of their children's classroom performance and behaviour and in this again their desires reflect those of pupils examined earlier. Many would also have welcomed more detailed advice on how they might help their child. In some cases parents pointed out that most of the report was concerned with negative criticism of performance and what was required was a far more positive approach indicating how the position might be rectified. Only 28 parents, however, considered that the report provided information which was unnecessary. The examples given were almost totally concerned with teachers' comments on a child's personality.

Heads were asked in the main survey if parents had expressed views supporting the reporting procedure or if they had suggested change. Over half of the head teachers provided examples of parental support for the system whereas less than ten per cent recorded that parents had suggested the introduction of change. A number of heads indicated that their comments did not necessarily mean that there had been any formal attempt to discover parental opinion, and many responded that they could not recall any reaction 'one way or the other'.

Aspects which most commonly gave rise to favourable comments, in addition to the provision of detailed information and advice, were the opportunity to reply, and the frequency of reports where these were provided at termly or half-termly intervals. Points requiring change were a mirror-image of these, being dominated by requests for more regular reports and for more detailed and individual comments. Among the six schools involved in the parent survey, in four, heads had recorded no reactions from parents either supportive or suggesting change. In School A, where a slip system was in use, the head recalled positive support concerning the individual nature of the comment which was provided, 'it looks as though the teachers care', and also approval for slight variations in the format of slips produced by teachers in the different subject disciplines. The head teacher of School F where reports were provided at a parents' evening, recorded that 'some parents have of course demanded that reports be sent home and that they should not be forced to collect them'. The same school had responded to parents' requests for individual slip reports.

Although parental opinion was seldom sought in any formal way a small number of schools provided the team with examples of their own work in this area. An example is provided in Appendix B4.

In the light of the more limited use of written reports in special schools parental reactions from this area were of particular interest. Supportive views were commonly claimed by head teachers and comments suggesting change were rather more rare than from ordinary schools. Where written reports were issued head teachers recorded that they 'gave the school status' in the parents' eyes and that parents liked receiving reports such as those from 'normal schools'. Where written reports were not provided some head teachers admitted that 'parents would like written reports but accept the present situation' and others pointed out that 'some parents desire a report on every tiny morsel of deviant behaviour'. Other heads recorded that parents approved of the personal contact involved in oral reporting:

> Many parents express relief that someone has spare time to listen to their side; reporting should be two way. Is it possible that the tradition of written reports has emerged because parents are unlikely to write back?

Discussions with pupils

Nine out of ten parents had retained their child's previous report and over three quarters recorded comparing the results of the present report with it. It was clear that parents considered the report an important item of discussion within the family circle – but not outside it. Only a quarter of the parents had talked about the most recent report with other parents from the school and the project team observed that at the parents' evenings little conversation between parents was concerned with the school report.

Ninety-five per cent of parents claimed to have discussed the report fully with their child when it reached the home, with only three per cent claiming that discussion was limited to the critical aspects of the report. The proportion contrasts with that claimed by the students, where only 44 per cent felt that the discussions with their parents had been 'detailed'. A similar disparity of perception occurred concerning the frequency of general discussions about work at school (Table 7.5). Here the proportion of parents claiming daily or weekly discussions about work in schools was more than double the proportion of students making the same claim.

Table 7.5: Frequency of discussions about school work in the home

Discussion about school work	Parent sample (N = 1,375) %	Pupil sample (N = 2,016) %
Very frequent (e.g. daily/weekly)	69	33
Often (e.g. every 2–3 weeks)	27	40
Infrequent (e.g. once a term)	4	27
Totals	100	100
Missing cases	22	34

Parents took a rather more optimistic view of the effect of the report than did teachers (see Chapter 6). Forty-six per cent expected that the report would produce a change in the way in which their child would work in school, 36 per cent felt that there would be a change in the way their child worked at home and 25 per cent thought that the report would bring about a change in their child's conduct at school. Twenty-two per cent of the parents considered that the report would have an effect on their own behaviour. Such changes fell into three main categories: increasing the supervision of homework; offering encouragement and help including specific tuition in areas of weakness;

and providing better facilities for home study. Although parents'
expectations of the effectiveness of the report in changing the working
pattern of their children might be greater than that expressed by
teachers, it was still considerably less than that of the majority of
pupils. Although it was possible to 'match' parent responses with those
of their children for only three quarters of the sample of 1,375 parents,
it is apparent from Table 7.6 that where pupils claim that the report
will bring about a change in the way they work at school, 44 per cent
of their parents did not expect this to occur. Where pupils had claimed
they would change their way of working at home, there was an even
greater discrepancy, with over half the parents recording that they
expected no change in their child's behaviour.

Table 7.6: Parents' and pupils' views concerning whether ways of
working will change as a result of the report

Pupils' claim	*Parents' expectation*		*Total*
	Will change	Will not change	
Will change way of working	425	340	765
Will not change way of working	59	209	268
Totals	484	549	1,033†

† N = 1,375; 'unmatched' cases: 342.

Discussions with teachers: the parents' evening

It was noted in Chapter 3 that reports were only one of several types
of contact schools had with parents and all except six ordinary schools
in the sample held parents' evenings with a reporting function. Special
schools, despite their lower level of provision of written reports,
contrasted strongly with this pattern, with over 40 per cent of them
making no formal provision for parent–teacher meetings concerned
with reporting. A higher proportion (27 as compared with 21 per cent)
of such schools did, however, provide parents' evenings not associated
with reporting.

Heads' estimates of attendance at parents' evenings are shown for
each school year group in Table 7.7. A pattern of declining attendance

Table 7.7: Heads' estimates of attendance at parents' evenings
associated with reporting (ordinary schools)

% Attendance (N:)	% of schools containing each year group						
	Year 1 (568)	Year 2 (598)	Year 3 (587)	Year 4 (554)	Year 5 (540)	Year 6 (328)	Year 7 (286)
0–25	1	3	–	3	4	2	2
26–50	9	15	13	29	25	7	7
51–75	29	45	40	44	42	30	31
76–99	59	37	46	23	28	57	57
100	1	1	1	1	1	4	3
Totals	99†	101†	100	100	100	100	100
Non-respondents	50	64	41	61	75	65	107

† Rounding error.

appeared to be broken upon the entry of the pupil to the sixth form,
with heads' estimates of attendance at this time approximating closely
to those for year one. Some heads pointed out that only those pupils
whose parents took an active interest in their education could hope to
reach the sixth form.

Estimates of attendance were available from only one third of heads
of special schools. There were, however, interesting departures from
the pattern found in ordinary schools. Low attendance was much more
common throughout but there was no evidence of the marked decline
in attendance associated with the age of the students which so characterized the pattern in ordinary schools.

Factors which were identified by head teachers as promoting
attendance included a high local interest in education, an active Parent–
Teacher Association and parental opportunity to select a secondary
school. Other less frequently mentioned factors were a small catchment
area and parents' availability due to local unemployment. Heads
identified a wider range of factors which they considered reduced
attendance, the most positive of which were that parents could visit
the school whenever they wished, that the school offered good informal
home–school relations and that the report provided adequate in-

formation. Other factors were concerned with the constraints of employment, such as shift work, the low value placed by parents on the importance of school, the presence of younger brothers or sisters in the family, a large catchment area and lack of transport. Additional information added by many of the heads indicated that high attendance figures were achieved largely as a result of considerable effort:

> The school goes out of its way — monthly clinics, monthly bulletins to parents, 'settling-in' reports for children who arrive during the year from other areas, social and educational PTA activities as opposed to purely fund-raising efforts — these encourage parents to see the education of their children as a matter for close collaboration.

The particular problem that parents with handicapped children have in finding 'sitters' was mentioned by a number of heads in special schools. In such schools non-attendance was, however, chiefly attributed to the large catchment areas, poor public transport and the opportunity which parents were offered to visit the school whenever they wished.

From the six schools which took part in the more intensive studies of pupils and parents, it was apparent that heads' estimates of attendance were fairly accurate, the tendency being to under- rather than over-estimate. The estimates of heads in these schools did not follow the general pattern indicating a decline in attendance as pupils progressed through the school. Nor did the proportion of parents expressing a wish to discuss the report with teachers decline with the age of the student. In all schools, however, the proportion of parents wishing to discuss reports with school staff was lowest in the second year, with just over one in five parents wanting discussion at this stage in one school (School C).

The general picture which emerged from the parents' questionnaires was that nearly two thirds of parents intended to visit the school and talk to staff about the report. Sixty-three per cent of those intending such visits wanted to see teachers of subjects where their child was not doing well, as compared with 54 per cent who wanted to contact teachers who had given a 'good' report. Sixty-eight per cent wished to talk to their child's form tutor, but in School F, where the *only* contact was with the form tutor, parents expressed a strong wish to meet the subject teachers, so that they could discuss progress in specific areas of the curriculum. Relatively few parents wished to discuss their child's report with the head, deputy head or heads of house or year. Such discussions appeared to be instituted when there was disagreement between parent and teacher or when a decision beyond the power of the subject teachers had to be reached. Typically, head teachers and senior teachers were involved in arbitration concerning option choice and examination entry.

School F was exceptional in that parents had to collect the report at the parents' evening, and this procedure was criticized in a number of responses. Some incomplete questionnaires were returned by parents who, due to personal circumstances, had been unable to see a report on their child's progress for several years. One such parent wrote:

> I cannot comment on getting reports from the school. I have two children and one or both have been going to the school since 1968 and I have never seen any of the reports since they started. I have written to the school many times asking if I could see the reports and then the children take them back. The school has never sent them to me.

The group tutor had written on the envelope containing the parent questionnaire:

> Mr and Mrs A. have never been able to get in from (a village on the edge of a large rural catchment) to collect any reports for Mary since she has been in the school.

Other parents returning questionnaires complained of the inflexibility of the system which failed to account for individual difficulties.

In another school where the same system was attempted, the head teacher underlined some of the problems. These started with 'disputes with the staff ('all that work for nothing'), continued with the writing of letters to all non-attending parents, 'attempting to set up another appointment', and concluded with the reports being sent home when, as the head teacher described it, 'my nerve had given way'.

Conversations with parents attending parents' evenings highlighted a number of issues. Most critical comments were focused upon the waiting time which characterized evenings not regulated by parent–teacher appointments. On several occasions parents pointed out that they had spent more than two hours awaiting their ten minute contact with the desired teacher. The duration of the interviews, which were sometimes as brief as five minutes, also provoked comment and parents were critical too of the lack of privacy, with meetings held *en masse* in school halls. Finally, a very small number of parents were concerned with what they saw as 'compulsory attendance' at an event of doubtful value. Although these parents felt that the discussions with teachers under the conditions outlined above were unlikely to prove fruitful they felt compelled to attend to avoid their child's progress in school being prejudiced.

All the 647 teachers in the sample were working in schools in which parents' evenings were held although a small proportion (three per cent) were from schools which only held evenings unconnected with reporting to parents. A further three per cent did not attend the reporting evenings which did occur. Teachers reported that most meetings lasted between two and three hours and involved them meeting almost 20 sets of parents. Teachers were almost evenly divided between those who discussed subject reports with parents and those who discussed both subject and tutorial reports. Very few were concerned in discussing only pastoral or tutorial reports. The length of the discussion with each set of parents varied between three and 23 minutes, with only one teacher spending an hour on a single discussion. The average time spent on each discussion was eight minutes.

Because teachers were asked to provide details of the total time spent at the evening, the number of parents with whom discussions were held and the duration of discussions, it was possible to estimate the non-contact time involved for each teacher. As might be expected there were considerable variations between teachers, with non-contact time varying from a few minutes to almost the whole meeting in some cases. Over half (54 per cent) of the teachers spent more than 30 minutes without seeing parents. Teachers of aesthetics and craft subjects, the humanities (other than English), modern and classical languages and the sciences recorded 'gaps' of more than 30 minutes less frequently than their colleagues, and English teachers, somewhat surprisingly, were most likely to pass time without parents (Table 7.8).

Although the most commonly expressed perception was that 'the parents we really want to see never come', few teachers identified the discussions as of little value. A tiny minority pointed out that parents' evenings were 'exhausting and demoralizing' and some of these considered most discussions a waste of time. A number of rather sceptical teachers complained that on occasions they had to 'defend their actions' and that discussion with parents was not much help in

Table 7.8: Subject specialist teachers recording more than 30
minutes without seeing parents

Subject	Subject teachers†	
	N	%
Aesthetics and craft	54	47
Commerce/business studies	14	61
English	52	69
Humanities other than English	50	48
Mathematics	45	57
Modern/classical languages	25	49
Physical education	17	59
Remedial education	15	56
Sciences	52	51

† Teachers offering more than one main subject are excluded from
this table.

resolving classroom-based problems. A contrasting view was that:
'Too many teachers are afraid to admit and discuss the problems
they are having with pupils — discussion benefits both parties', and
teachers commonly saw the evenings with parents as useful. The benefits
teachers identified can be considered as grouping themselves in four
areas. The first concerns contact — often the only contact which teachers
had with parents. Second is the gaining of information, where the
major benefits were identified as obtaining new knowledge about the
students and their backgrounds. Features that were commonly
mentioned included the gaining of additional information about parent
and student aspirations and ambitions and details of previously unknown
handicaps or unsuspected difficulties as well as details of home and
family background which were seen as contributing to or causing
problems within the school.

The third area centred on the opportunity to 'improve' the report
by means of discussion. This was referred to by some teachers as
being able 'to pass on information which cannot be written on reports'
whereas others saw it as 'good to be able to back up comments'. A
number of teachers explained that they felt happier giving verbal
comments and welcomed the opportunity to amplify the somewhat
attenuated comment possible on even the largest of reports and to
provide suitable examples from their classroom experience to explain

what their report comment or the grade had meant − 'one can achieve far more and make far more positive comment than one can in a banal, cliched report'.

The fourth area of comment was concerned with establishing relationships with parents, building up trust and interest and, as one teacher commented, 'introducing an element of human warmth into a professional relationship'. Teachers contributing comments in this group used phrases indicating a concern to 'solicit parental support', 'gain parental cooperation' and bring about parents' 'active participation' in the work of the school.

The most comprehensive statement of the advantages of discussion with parents was provided by a highly experienced humanities teacher; because it covers points raised by many teachers and reverberates with an enthusiasm for the possibilities of parent−teacher dialogue, it is quoted in full:

> It (i.e. discussion with parents) enables teachers to make a much fuller report than is possible in writing: answer queries that arise, and engage in a meaningful dialogue with parents so that any problems may be clarified and tackled jointly. Teachers can also gain much from meeting the parents and in a conversation it is possible to assess how much information/criticism can be transmitted: it is also possible to learn about the home background, the amount of support one can expect, e.g. *re* dress, homework and the like. The student's problems can also be discussed in greater detail, and often one evokes a greater degree of empathy − and sympathy − from these meetings. The students feel that they are important as individuals, not merely ciphers, or one of a class. Parents can assess the attitude of teachers; clarify misunderstandings, e.g. ambiguity in reports; discover the areas where the child needs most help; avoid or reduce tension/personality clashes and request changes. Pupils also recognise that (in the main) parents and teachers are co-operating in the education of the children. Other teachers find similar advantages, probably the most important are those which usually ensue from personal contact − a sharing of insights and exchange of information, often at a more personal level than is possible by formal letter writing . . .

Teachers rarely criticized the organization of parents' evenings. Waiting and queueing, the two most common parents' grievances, received little mention. Many heads recorded an appointments system at parents' evenings to avoid the build-up of long queues of parents waiting to see the subject specialists. More than a third of schools, however, never used an appointment system and others recorded using it only 'on some occasions' — commonly for parents' evenings associated with third-year options, and fifth-year meetings prior to public examinations. None of the teachers' comments was concerned with another of the parents' grievances — lack of privacy to hold a discussion where considerable frankness as well as tact might be called for. In only two of the schools visited did parent–teacher discussion take place with any degree of privacy, although a number of schools in writing to the project stressed the importance they placed on this, with one school utilizing all available office space for this purpose.

The last issue to be discussed concerning parents' evenings is the attendance of pupils. Heads were asked if students were (a) permitted and (b) encouraged to attend parents' evenings. Their responses indicated that although two thirds of the schools allowed students to attend parents' evenings (Table 7.9) in far fewer were they encouraged to do so. Where attendance was 'in some cases' permitted and/or encouraged this most commonly related to two specific events; the evening devoted to option choice in year three and the evening preceding the finalization of entrance for public examinations. Occasional attendance by students

Table 7.9: School policy on student attendance at parents' evenings (ordinary|schools)†

	% students	
School policy	Permitted to attend	Encouraged to attend
Student attendance:		
In no cases	32	61
In some cases	34	24
In all cases	34	15
Totals	100	100
Non-respondents	20	29

† N = 740.

at parents' evenings might also be unrelated to reporting as, for example, in the case of 'pre-sixth-form' evenings and social events. Some schools recorded that they encouraged attendance in the sixth form.

Table 7.10 indicates a strong relationship between type of school and the policy adopted towards student attendance at parents' evenings. The 21 technical and 'other' schools together with the comprehensive schools tended to permit student attendance more frequently than grammar schools, while middle schools offered fewest opportunities for student participation — reflecting no doubt the age range of the pupils.

Table 7.10: School policy concerning student attendance at parents' evenings, shown by type of school† ††

	Middle/ secondary %	Comprehensive %	Secondary modern %	Grammar %	Technical and other %
Students permitted to attend:					
On no occasions	61	25	34	46	27
On some occasions	24	36	30	51	23
On all occasions	16	40	35	3	50
Totals	101†††	101†††	99†††	100	100

† A chi-square test performed on the data in this table yielded a value of $\chi^2 = 71.24$ which with eight degrees of freedom is significant beyond the .001 level.

†† N = 740; non-respondents: 20.

††† Rounding error.

Teachers' comments on student attendance at parents' evenings suggested that this was a relatively rare occurrence, even in some cases 'an unexplored area'. Where teachers had experienced the attendance of student and parent together they were not always convinced of the value of the exercise, perhaps because, although present, students were not necessarily seen as participants:

It is a false situation if they are present. It is often an embarrassment for them to hear people talk *about* them instead of *to* them. Occasionally a fruitful discussion can ensue but it is rare.

Other teachers pointed out:

> Students can be spoken to with parents present in a different atmos-
> phere to the normal school situation. Both parents and students
> are presented with the same facts allowing no room for misunder-
> standing or misreporting.

Some specified that it was essential for the student to 'take an
active part in the discussion', and recorded their appreciation of the
adult 'out-of-school' atmosphere; but many teachers described their
difficulty in discussing the situation 'honestly' in front of the student.
Of the heads who commented, a small number said they were unable
to accommodate students at parents' evenings because of shortage of
space, but much more commonly student attendance was considered
unproductive.

Discussions between students and members of the research team
suggested that in many cases they were quite fearful of the consequences
of parents and teachers meeting and even at sixth-form level a majority
talked of awaiting their parents' return from a parent–teacher evening
with apprehension. Limited observations of such meetings attended by
students indicated that many found if difficult to participate fully,
most sitting silently, while their parents dominated the discussion.

Usually, then, parent–teacher discussions were conducted in the
absence of the student and the value for the student was seen as related
to the accuracy of the parents' 'reporting back' and on the acceptance
by the parent of the teacher's point of view: 'if the parents support
the teacher the student benefits'.

Whatever the frustrations associated with parents' evenings – and it
is clear that these existed for both parents and teachers – it is apparent
that they provided the opportunity for parents to get information
from the sources they valued most. In their questionnaire parents
were asked to rank a series of sources of information into first, second
and third choices. To obtain from this a clear overview of the relative
importance of the sources selected, first choices were allocated three
points, second choices two and third choices one point. The results
are shown on Table 7.11 and indicate that parents rated talking to
subject teachers most highly of all, followed by talking to their child.
The school report came third, followed by discussions with form
tutors. Relatively little value was attached to talking to heads, deputy
heads, or house or year tutors, underlining the earlier finding that the

Table 7.11: Parents' preferred source of information concerning their child's progress in school

Source of information†	Points allocated	Rank order
Talking to subject teachers	2,344	1
Talking to child	2,059	2
Reading school report	1,535	3
Talking to form tutors	989	4
Talking to house/year tutors	468	5
Talking to head teacher/deputy head	207	6

† Although all parents could indicate three choices, 102 failed to indicate a second choice and 155 indicated no third choice.

comments of these teachers are not generally seen as being as useful as those of specialists in particular disciplines.

The parental reply slip

We conclude by considering briefly a further means offered in many schools for parents to communicate their views on their child's progress to the school: the parental reply slip. In this context we include a small exercise carried out by the project which explored parent replies in one school.

Perhaps the first point to be made here concerns the disappointment recorded by a number of heads at the low level of response from parents. In the school studied the proportion of parents returning the slip never exceeded one third and in the fifth year, once the period of compulsory education was nearly completed, hardly any parents responded. The reasons for parental non-response are not known. One possibility is that most parents are generally satisfied with their child's progress and see no need to comment; in the total sample of 1,375 parents for example, 30 per cent recorded being very satisfied with their child's progress, 40 per cent 'satisfied', with only seven per cent 'not at all satisfied'. Other possible explanations may relate to a simple reluctance to put pen to paper, or a feeling that perhaps no great attention would be given to their comments — but this is clearly an area where further study must replace conjecture.

It was quite clear from the analysis of parents' replies that the reply slip has considerable potential as a vehicle for different kinds of communication from parents to teachers, and a number of quite distinctive approaches were identified.

First, a large number were from parents who were pleased with their child's progress and wished to express their thanks to the school:

> I am very pleased with Sandra's progress. I can certainly see that she works very hard and I do hope this will continue. I am very grateful to all the teachers who help her. Thank you very much.

The opportunity to express gratitude in this way could well lead to such parents feeling that they need not attend parent—teacher consultations, thus relieving some pressure on what is usually an overcrowded meeting.

Almost as frequent were expressions of disappointment or concern:

> I am very much disappointed with Lorrain's work and behaviour. I only hope that she will pull herself together in the future.

> I have read Sharon's report and I was not pleased with her. I am worried about her misbehaviour in school, so if she is not good please let me know. I hope to be able to discuss Sharon when I see you.

Some parents suggested solutions:

> I am very disappointed with Roger's reports. I would like him to move away from Dwight and Charlie. I spoke to him and advised him about his homework. I hope to see him having science and maths homework.

More commonly, parents needed help in understanding their child:

> We, like you, are most disappointed with this report. We had hoped for a lot of improvement which is not there. We are at a loss to know how to get through to him — bribery, threats, promises. We have tried everything we can think of but with no success. All we can hope now is that his own commonsense will come to the top and he will buckle down.

Peter is a very good boy at home . . . so there is not much I can say because the report and the Peter I know are really two different people.

A few parents defended their child and placed any blame squarely upon the school:

... When I send my child to school I send her to learn and get discipline. You do not have to bully a child to have good discipline but it seems that you do not pay enough attention to the children. . . . In the circumstances you cannot blame the child.

It would have been fascinating indeed to have been able to document how such comments were followed up by the school.

In many further replies parents offered to supervise and to help with homework and make greater attempts to improve attendance and punctuality. Some parents asked questions about the content of the lessons, about the curriculum in general and about the sort of assessments of progress which were made. The picture that emerges is that here is a means of communication, which has considerable possibilities for developing a dialogue with those parents, albeit relatively few in number, who choose to take the opportunities the reply slip system offers.

Summary and discussion

Again, the findings in this chapter provide grounds for optimism. Most parents saw the report as useful and said they learned something new about their child's progress from it. Well over three quarters considered it gave a fair and accurate picture (though not necessarily a complete one), and clearly the report was something that was retained for future comparison. All but five per cent of parents claimed to have discussed the report fully with their child (many more than their children's evidence reported in Chapter 6 would suggest) and a substantial proportion, 46 per cent, expected that their child's way of working at school would change as a result of it. Over one in five parents intended to change their own behaviour, in terms of providing supervision, encouragement and better facilities for study. As in the last chapter, the possibilities of the report as a means of bringing about desired change are apparent, if only ways can be found of nourishing the intentions born at the time of its receipt.

While parents were largely satisfied with the information they received on aspects such as their child's progress in individual subjects, and their child 'as a person', there were areas where the need for more information was felt. Parents wanted fuller description of what their child had learned, together with more information concerning the nature of the teaching group he or she was placed in. The pupils' pleas for more information on their chances in public examinations were echoed by parents as was the call for more guidance concerning career and further education prospects. Parents' responses paralleled those of their children in other ways — for example in requests for more specific recommendations concerning remediation. Parents needed to know what they and their children were meant to do to effect any desired improvements. As with the pupils, ipsative assessment, whereby a child's performance was compared with his own previous work, was that most preferred by parents, although there was considerable mismatch between sets of parents and their children on the method of assessment each desired.

The chapter explored several issues associated with parents' evenings. Such evenings featured in all but a few schools, with parents' attendance influenced by factors such as the availability of public and private transport, the nature of the catchment area and parents' working commitments. A general decline in attendance was noted after the first year, which was not reversed until after the years of statutory education were completed. There was some indication, however, that sustained effort by schools in approaching the area of home–school relations from a variety of angles met with success in terms of increased parental attendance. In contrast, attempts at making attendance compulsory, by denying parents access to the report unless they visited the school to collect it, were fraught with difficulty.

Both teachers and parents saw parents' evenings as a useful activity. Given the low take-up by parents of the opportunity to give their comments on parental reply slips, the parents' evening provided in most instances the major means by which schools could obtain parents' reactions to the report. Teachers valued the opportunity to establish personal contact, to acquire new insights and information concerning their pupils, to expand and interpret the comments they had written on the report and to work in partnership with parents in furthering their child's development. Parents, for their part, particularly welcomed the opportunity to talk with their preferred sources of information, the subject specialists. The main problem for parents — which teachers seemed in some cases unaware of — concerned lack of privacy for discussions and having to queue for often brief interviews with the teachers they wanted to see. Problems of space clearly vary greatly from school to school and may not always be resolvable. However, it was apparent that some schools were finding at least partial solutions by using available office space for parental interviews, and many were able to minimize the problem of long waits by operating an appointments system. It was clear that some teachers spent a considerable amount of time at parents' evenings without seeing parents, and over half had more than 30 minutes of such 'free time'. Given, however, that an estimated 20 sets of parents were commonly seen in a meeting lasting between two to three hours, such 'free time' could in some cases provide very necessary breathing space.

Student attendance was allowed, at least on some occasions, in about two thirds of the schools, and was more common in comprehensive and technical schools than in grammar schools and extremely rare in middle schools. Less than half the schools reported *encouraging* it in any year group and evidence from teachers suggested that it was in fact relatively infrequent and most commonly was associated with evenings held at critical choice-points, such as in the third and fifth years. Discussing students' progress or lack of it with their parents could be a delicate task requiring skills and practice which many teachers — particularly those at the beginning of their careers — might well lack. A three-way dialogue in which the pupil, too, participates is likely to be even more demanding and it is not surprising that some teachers expressed negative views of the value of such encounters.

Chapter Eight

Developments in Reporting

Jackson (1971) introduced a study of 365 school reports with the observation that 'Surely no other aspect of school life has changed so little over twenty — or should it be fifty — years?' Our evidence suggests that this claim is no longer true even if it were so at the time. In this chapter we start by exploring the extent of changes in recent years and then go on to consider in some detail developments identified in the course of the project. As will become apparent, these range from relatively simple modifications of fairly common types of reporting practice to forms of reporting which may be regarded as more truly innovative.

Recent changes in reporting systems

Heads' responses to a question concerning how long the current report system in their schools had been in use are shown in Table 8.1. It is apparent from this that a considerable amount of change had taken place comparatively recently, with 53 per cent of schools having reporting systems less than five years old and only 12 per cent recording systems aged ten years or more.

In the five years preceding the survey 16 per cent of ordinary schools had increased the number of reports issued annually, as compared with 14 per cent which had decreased it. Changes in staff responsibilities, such as the delegation of tasks previously undertaken by the head, had occurred in 34 per cent of schools, and changes in the system of marking or grading in 46 per cent. The most commonly reported change, however, related to type of report and this was recorded in

Table 8.1: The age of current report systems

Age of system	Ordinary schools (N=740) %	Special schools (N=97) %
Less than 1 year	9	10
1–4 years	44	40
5–9 years	34	31
10 years or more	12	16
Don't know	1	2
Totals	100	99†
Non-respondents	4	8

† Rounding error.

nearly two thirds of schools (Table 8.2). The major trend was the introduction of the slip system in place of single sheets or report books (Table 8.3). The main reasons given by heads for introducing changes in report type were the need to provide more space for teachers to comment and to give parents more information such as a slip system allowed (Table 8.4). A wish to provide parents with an opportunity to respond was cited as an important factor by 43 per cent of the schools introducing change, indicating an increased emphasis by schools on ways of bringing parents more fully into the reporting process. About a fifth of heads cited reasons such as the avoidance of queuing or the 'halo effect' — again advantages closely associated with the slip system.

Where the type of report had been changed, changes applied in two thirds of cases to all year groups. In the remaining schools, changes were limited to certain years and further examples of changes affecting selected year groups included the introduction of 'settling in' reports after a pupil had transferred to the school, the provision of predictive grading prior to public examinations and the production of leaving profiles for non-examination candidates.

Many schools cited examples of changes in the preceding five years

Table 8.2: Major changes in the reporting system in the
preceding five years

The nature of the change in the reporting system†	Ordinary schools (N=740) %	Special schools (N=97) %
An increase in the number of reports issued annually	16	18
A decrease in the number of reports issued annually	14	8
A change in staff responsibilities, e.g. delegation	34	20
A change in the system of marking or grading	46	6
A change in the type of report	63	13

† Some schools made more than one type of change.

Table 8.3: Changes in the last five years — the new report and the
report which it replaced (ordinary schools)

Type of report	Report introduced (N=465) %	Report replaced (N=444)† %
Single sheet	28	48
Slip system	58	7
Report book	12	45
Letter	2	—
Totals	100	100

† Twenty-one schools did not supply information on the nature of the
report which had been replaced.

Table 8.4: The reasons for introducing a new report

Reasons for change†	Schools (N=465) %
To allow more space for teacher comment	77
To provide parents with more detailed information about the pupil (grades/marks)	69
To provide space for parent reply	43
To provide parents with more information about the school (e.g. grouping policy)	31
To avoid type-specific problems, e.g. halo effect, teacher queuing	21
To provide school with a duplicate copy	7
To meet change in school, e.g. reorganization	5
Other reasons	7

† Some schools gave more than one reason for introducing change.

which they did not consider constituted a change in the type of report used. These included such changes as the replacement of carbon paper for duplication by a report printed on NCR paper, the introduction of pastoral or tutorial reports, minor changes in format, changes in response to alteration in the option subjects offered in the upper school, the provision of reports in Welsh and English, an increased emphasis on oral reporting and the provision of additional progress reports, usually in the form of grade cards issued at the end of the first term or in mid year.

When completing their questionnaires a number of heads expressed their dissatisfaction with the system of reports currently in use. Some also provided examples of factors which inhibited the introduction of any improvements. The most frequently quoted reason for maintaining an unsatisfactory system was the cost of changing and this was particularly the case in schools holding large stocks of reports, resulting from previous attempts to obtain the most favourable unit price. One head teacher recounted woefully that having just taken over his 'new' school he discovered in various cupboards around the building sufficient report books, of rather outmoded design, to provide for the reporting needs of the school for the next seven years. Staff reluctance to change was also an issue raised by a small number of head teachers who suspected that forcing through a major change against the wishes of a large proportion of the staff was bound to fail.

Despite such difficulties, over a fifth of the heads of ordinary schools indicated that they expected changes to occur in the reporting system within the next academic year and in special schools the figure was one in three. The most common expected changes were the introduction of a new report or a change in layout of the existing report. In almost one third of the ordinary schools where heads were expecting changes, these concerned the system of grading. The introduction of space for parental comment was mentioned in both ordinary and special schools.

Examples of innovation

Despite the limited range of report types currently in common use, the project was provided with a number of less common reports and with examples of novel reporting practices. The intention in the paragraphs which follow is to describe these; it should not, however, be inferred that they are necessarily examples of 'good practice'.

The examples fall into three main groups. The first consists essentially of modifications of commonly used report types; the second are developments to meet specialist functions, responding, for example, to differences in age or subject matter; and the third group comprise more fundamental innovations.

i.   Modifications

CONTINUITY AND SPACE
Since each of the common types of report clearly has both advantages and difficulties, a number of schools had introduced reports which were essentially a compromise between the alternatives. The three examples described in this section were all modifications of the slip system.

In one school an attempt to overcome the problem of a lack of continuity had been made. Each subject slip provided for two reports: one for the first half of the academic year and one for the second.

Pastoral reports were similarly divided. As well as making comparison with the previous report easier for both teacher and parent, teachers no longer needed to spend time writing the pupil's name, the subject and the form when the slip was used for the second report. The slips were conveyed to and from home in a folder which could be used throughout the pupil's school life, and parents were urged to remove and retain reports once both sections for any year had been completed.

The remaining two examples focused on the problem of the excessive area of paper to be filled in the slip system by teachers who may have little to report. In both cases individual subject slips were replaced by slips each dealing with a number of subjects grouped to provide 'logical' clusters, such as aesthetic and craft subjects and the sciences. Such a format allowed different amounts of space to be allocated for individual subjects. In one case, for example, art received twice the space allocated to the craft subjects. The modified system had the disadvantage, commonly associated with the single sheet report, of teachers waiting for others to complete the report and also introduced the possibility of halo effects. In both cases, however, only a limited number of teachers would be involved.

Because commercial constraints tended to impose a rather bland uniformity of appearance, reports making the most imaginative use of space were often produced within the school. With many schools having sophisticated printing facilities this did not result in an unprofessional-looking product but, where suitable quality card or paper was used, provided a distinctive and functional report. Such school-produced reports also avoided the problems which arose when a report had to be ordered in massive quantities in order to obtain a low unit cost.

GRADING

A number of schools provided examples of modifications concerned with grading and we start by looking briefly at the tiny group of four ordinary schools which rejected grading on reports altogether. Clearly critical in this situation is the attitude of parents, who might well expect some comparative information. Questioned on this point, one of the heads pointed out that:

Our systems have been established for so long that if parents felt strongly about the lack of comparative information they would have felt this many years ago. We do still receive one or two queries each year (out of some fifteen hundred reports) but certainly there is no evidence at present that parents have some avid desire for an overall grade.

The same head believed that reporting without grades encouraged a greater value being placed on the comments by both the teacher writing and the parent reading the report. The reports were said to result in a considerable dialogue between all the interested parties, including the pupils. Where clear indications of future examination performances were required the school relied on the subject teacher to make this information available in their comments.

A staff memorandum on 'standards' produced in another school linked non-grading with a decision by the staff to introduce mixed ability teaching:

> Certain other decisions arising from the central mixed ability decision had to be faced by the staff. These decisions concerned grading, reports, etc. On this matter the staff were almost equally united. It was agreed to do away with marks and gradings recognising that they would create very considerable injustices in the mixed ability situation and be counter-productive in the improvement in school atmosphere which we expected to be a by-product of the reorganisation and which all our reactions to our present third and fourth years suggest is being achieved.
>
> Reports and assessments now eschew the easy way out of a grading based on a many-point scale and require a descriptive and hopefully analytic comment. This we hope to see eventually build a profile of each pupil, more individual and worthwhile than the sort of assessment we used to have.

More commonly, schools' modifications to their grading systems had the aim of overcoming the limited nature of the information conveyed by a single grade. In such schools the aspects of work and behaviour assessed by grades were increased as in the four examples which follow:

School 1   (Graded A – E for each subject.)
(a) Mastery of basic skills.
(b) Attitude in class.
(c) Homework.

School 2   (Graded A – E for each subject.)
(a) Presentation.
(b) Attitude.
(c) Content.

School 3   (Graded A – E for each subject.)
(a) Apparent interest in subject.
(b) Effort in classwork.
(c) Home/individual study.
(d) Practical/manipulative skills (graded within teaching group).
(e) Standard of written work (graded within teaching group).
(f) Overall standard of work (compared with the whole age group).

School 4   (Provided in addition to an *overall* five-point normative attainment grade in each subject.)
(a) Attainment. One indicated from:
Quick to understand new work. Learns slowly but remembers well. Understands but with difficulty. Understands little of the work.
(b) Attitude. One indicated from:
Shows initiative and works well. Always works to best of ability. Sometimes works to best of ability. Makes little effort. Lacks interest.

Other behaviours were routinely graded and reported on within each subject context in a number of schools and these included grammatical accuracy, logical thinking, understanding and interpretation, the gaining of factual knowledge, capability, persistence in learning or other work, and originality and the production of imaginative ideas.

Three schools, while not extending the range of behaviours which were graded, provided assessments in figurative form. In one instance, such assessments were made on a line marked 'below 30' at one end and '90' at the other; in another, a line marked at equal divisions with 'More able', 'Average' and 'Less able' was used. The student's position was indicated by shading an area on the line and instructions to teachers suggested shading not more than one fifth of the line. This can be seen, then, as a visual representation of a five-point scale. Although such a system theoretically provided no extra information for the student or the parent it was claimed that it drew attention to the fact that assessments were not precise measures and should be interpreted as giving only estimates of attainment.

PARENTAL REPLY SLIPS

The reluctance of parents to take advantage of the opportunity schools offered to comment on their child's report was noted in the last chapter. The analysis of reports sent to the project (see Chapter 2) indicated that while most of the schools inviting parents to reply had a space, or in some cases a whole page, headed 'Parents' comments', others adopted a more positive and encouraging approach. Examples of such attempts ranged from printed phrases such as, 'I would like to add my own comments on this report and on my child's general progress at school:' to the provision of a special booklet for parents which included the following statement from the head teacher:

> You can also play your part by completing the back page of the report and returning it to school as soon as possible. We really do want to hear from you, so please take advantage of the space provided. Your comments on the report itself — its style and content, or any aspect of your child's education would be welcome.
>
> There is no doubt in my mind that pupils make better progress when parents show interest in the school.

Another school provided a questionnaire:

Parents Report Please would you tick the appropriate box and add your comments.

1. I am pleased with my child's progress:

    Yes ☐   Not sure ☐   No ☐

2. I am pleased with my child's happiness at school:

    Yes ☐   Not sure ☐   No ☐

3. The amount of homework done is:

    Too much ☐   About right ☐   Not enough ☐

4. Please add any other comments or questions.

Some of the schools providing invitations to parents' evenings with the school report applied similar methods of encouragement, and some also accompanied the report with a 'tick list' of staff whom parents wished to consult. The completed list was circulated to the staff involved, appointment times were allocated and a timetable of consultations sent back to parents.

The effectiveness of such inducements to parental involvement could not be assessed in the course of the project, but they merit attention as examples of attempts actively to promote parental response and involvement in an area where many schools have found it lacking.

ii. Reports with specialist functions

A number of schools provided examples of reports which served specific needs: induction reports or reports for pupils in particular year groups; interim reports mid term or mid year (often in the form of grade cards); monitoring or supervising reports, used as a punitive measure or as an aid to individual assessment; reports responding to differences in ability or subject content; and leaving reports, including leaver profiles.

INDUCTION REPORTS AND REPORTS FOR DIFFERENT AGE GROUPS

As noted in Chapter 2, just under half the schools surveyed provided different reports for different year groups and a few provided induction reports for those who had recently joined the school. In general, induction reports took the form of a letter, sometimes prestructured, from the form tutor. Subject teachers were seldom involved and often this first report was aimed more at initiating dialogue with parents than at imparting information on progress. A few more detailed exceptions were sent to the project. By way of example, one of these included:

(a) Space for form teachers' comments.
(b) Space for comments specifically related to attendance, punctuality, uniform, attitude to adults, attitude to work and responsibility.
(c) An indication of participation in school activities (tick list).
(d) Space for comments by subject teachers.
(e) A report from the year tutor.

This report was given to parents at the end of the first half of the first term and was the subject of a subsequent parents' evening.

Changes in report format were frequently introduced after the third year, with named subject spaces becoming less common in order to cater for the flexibility of the option system. Reports for senior years might also include predictions of public examination performance, though it is clear from the preceding chapters that this did not occur as frequently as parents or pupils would wish. An example of unusually specific information occurred on the fifth-form report slips in one school where teachers gave a prediction of the grades expected and, in addition, answered the following questions:

Will he/she benefit from staying on?
Could he/she in your subject progress to an 'A' level course?
Has he/she probably reached maximum level?

REPORTS FOR SCHOOL LEAVERS
It should first be noted that, unlike other forms of reporting that we have considered, the audience for leaver reports was seen as comprising employers rather than parents. A number of schools provided the project with examples of leaving reports or formalized leaving testimonials and others wrote of their experimentation with the Swindon Record of Personal Achievement (Schools Council, 1979) or with their own version of the self-report framework for non-examination candidates. Appendix B5 provides a description of the materials used in the RPA scheme and a comment on its rationale. A visit by members of the team to a school using a modified version of the Swindon Profiling System confirmed a number of points raised by other schools.

The modification had been introduced to reduce costs and was used for those fifth formers 'who would normally be very difficult' and who would have 'little chance of getting a job'. They were described as 'falling into the grey area, those not taking 'O' level or many CSEs but not those from within the remedial group'. The students followed a community-oriented work-experience scheme centred upon local homes, hospitals and similar community provision. Their programmes were practically based, involving a minimum of written work, although students kept their own folder of work which included a day-to-day record of their visits and activities. Recording was largely a matter of their own initiative although teaching staff checked the folders of work: 'if they don't want to say anything they don't'.

At the end of the course students were provided with a leaving certificate which detailed their participation in the scheme and focused on factors such as trustworthiness, attitude and punctuality.

As the team completed the research phase of the work they were provided with a document, collaboratively produced by the staff of seven secondary schools and one technical college which recorded the collective view that:

(a) Although the need for leaving certificates had been generated by experience with pupils who are least able and/or least motivated in the present system, it was recommended that any procedure for reporting should apply to the whole of the school leaving population.

(b) It was agreed that the prime requirement of any report should be its educational validity but that it should reflect the needs and demands of employers. It was felt that a scheme which both improved and commented on the personal development of the individual pupil would be welcomed by responsible employers. Thus it was recommended that close consultation needed to be developed and maintained with selected local employers.

(c) It was recommended that the scheme implemented should be a profile reporting system based on a model such as the scheme developed by the Scottish Council for Research in Education, (1977) but modified extensively to meet local needs. It was felt that the profile could be built up during the pupil's time in the fourth and fifth years and that pupils would be involved in discussion about the development of the profile so that learning/improving possibilities could be worked on a tutorial basis.

The provisional framework for a leaver's profile report which resulted from the deliberations of the group is given in Figure 8.1. This report was identified as a confidential document which would be 'made available to employers and other interested parties by photocopy or direct copying onto another report blank'.

Other examples produced by schools carried less structured information although one school included subject grades on a nine-point scale covering the three previous years, together with examination results, and suggested that the draft for the leaver's testimonial should be completed after reference to:

(a) the student progress form (an internal school record);
(b) the school reports to parents;
(c) the personal development form (an internal school record);
(d) the student interest form (self-report);
(e) student career interests at time of testimonial;
(f) progress records from link courses, work experience or out of school activities and achievements.

A further example included criterion-graded information on 60 language, mathematical, practical, personal and social skills, including several aspects of potential use to an employer such as typing speed and 'understanding' of value added tax 'Teacher and student reactions to a range of such learning profiles are explored in Goacher (1983).

REPORTS FOR PUPILS OF DIFFERENT ABILITIES
A small number of schools gave reports of a different type to pupils according to their ability. Most commonly this consisted of the elimination of normative data from the reports of the less able. In one case less able children were given a letter from their remedial teacher rather than the conventional subject-oriented single sheet report provided for the rest of the school.

A further school produced a single sheet report of slightly different format for 'more able' students. The standard report provided an A — E grade for 'Assessment', 'Effort' and 'Conduct', whereas parents of 'more able' students received a judgement of 'Good', 'Satisfactory' or 'Unsatisfactory' in two areas, 'Attainment' and 'Homework'. The standard report was printed commercially while the 'more able' report was produced within the school. Unfortunately, no clear reasons for the differences between the reports were offered by the school and it can only be surmised that the concentration on academic achievement (rather than effort and conduct) together with the brief uncompromising verbal description of it, was intended to make the identification of those failing to fulfil their potential an easier task.

Another school, while not carrying out different reporting strategies, gave details of a scheme for monitoring the progress of the 'most able'. The material is considered appropriate for inclusion here, since its stated objective was to involve 'pupil, *parents*, subject teacher, form teacher, year tutor and deputy head'. Its emphasis on dialogue between teacher and pupil in the monitoring process is of particular interest in view of the difficulties in this area noted in Chapter 6.

Figure 8.1: *Leaver's profile report: provisional framework*

PUNCTUALITY
1. Can always be relied upon to arrive on time.
2. Can be relied upon to arrive on time for most occasions.
3. Cannot be relied upon to arrive on time.

ATTENDANCE
1. Completely satisfactory.
2. Some record of absence.
3. Significant absences from school.

RELIABILITY
1. Always reliable.
2. Normally reliable.
3. Unreliable.

PERSEVERANCE
1. Usually undeterred by difficulties.
2. Conscientious in approach to a problem.
3. Makes reasonable efforts to overcome difficulties.
4. Will make some effort if frequently encouraged.
5. Rarely makes an effort.

USE OF NUMBER
1. Quick and accurate.
2. Can handle routine calculations with practice.
3. Can barely cope with simple calculations.

USE OF SPOKEN LANGUAGE
1. Speaks clearly and confidently with good vocabulary.
2. Capable of reasonable expression with minimum of hesitation.
3. Finds difficulty in speaking in complete sentences, hesitates and has limited vocabulary.

UNDERSTANDING OF SPEECH
1. Understands complex discussion and instructions.
2. Understands most discussion and instructions.
3. Has difficulty in understanding discussion and instructions often need repeating.

INITIATIVE
1. Shows clear initiative in most situations.
2. Shows clear initiative if given a little guidance.
3. Works along defined guidelines with prompting.
4. Needs regular guidance.
5. No initiative and needs constant guidance to continue work.

ABILITY TO WORK WITH OTHERS
1. Makes full contribution and takes leadership role.
2. Makes full contribution with high level cooperation.
3. Prefers to be directed by others but works well.
4. Cannot always be relied upon to cooperate.
5. Very rarely cooperative.

READING ABILITY
1. Can understand complex written material.
2. Can understand all everyday written material.
3. Limited understanding of simple material.

WRITING
1. Writes accurately and lucidly.
2. Competent with everyday spelling and grammar.
3. Experiences difficulty with most aspects of written work.

ARTISTIC/CREATIVE
1. Capable of understanding appropriate concepts and uses materials sympathetically.
2. Produces sound work but may need help with new challenges or concepts.
3. Needs constant assistance.

MANUAL DEXTERITY
1. Highly skilled in use of hands.
2. Skill level satisfactory.
3. Has limited powers of dexterity.

CURRICULUM KNOWLEDGE AND INTEREST

Subjects
and Level

	1.		2.		3.	
4.		5.		6.		7.
8.		9.		10.		11.

Notes

HEALTH AND GENERAL FITNESS

OVERALL COMMENTS

During a three-week monitoring period each 'most able' student was allocated a member of staff to supervise the process. Parents were involved in a scrutiny of homework and could comment on all aspects of the homework being undertaken. Staff commented on three areas: lessons, homework and school life and the student completed a lesson assignment which after a brief description of the work attempted sought comments as follows:

(a) I enjoyed it very much.
(b) I thought it OK.
(c) I did not enjoy the lesson.

(a) I understood all the work.
(b) I understood some of the work.
(c) I understood very little of the work.

(a) The work was very difficult.
(b) The work was not too difficult.
(c) The work was easy.

(a) Most of my work was listening to teacher.
(b) Most of my work was writing.
(c) Most of my work was reading.
(d) My work was an equal proportion of time:
   i. listening to teacher/writing
   ii. writing/reading
   iii. listening to teacher/reading
   iv. listening to teacher/writing/reading
(e) Most of my time was spent doing none
    of these. (State what you did.)

Do you think that you could have worked harder?   YES
   NO

done more work?   YES
   NO

The process was completed by an interview with the student where the supervisor was urged:

Try to help the student relax and talk honestly. Do *not* dwell on any comments she/he makes relating to staff — in fact make it clear that staff names must *not* be used . . . The question 'why' seems appropriate, e.g. why did you enjoy the lesson? Other aspects to be pursued: worries and problems; extra-curricular activities; what the student does in form time; what the student would like to exist in school which does not and ways in which the student would like to improve the school.

In another school a report which was specifically intended to be motivational had been developed by a head of department and consisted of a teacher-to-student report for 'O' level students. This was intended to provide the students with 'detailed advice' and to encourage 'realistic feedback' from students to staff. There appeared to be some confusion, however, on the part of various departmental staff concerning its purpose and application and this perhaps highlights the difficulties which those seeking to develop more structured teacher—pupil dialogue about reports are likely to face.

REPORTS FOR DIFFERENT SUBJECTS

In Chapter 5 it was noted that a third of the teachers identified subject-specific problems concerned with assessing and reporting; few examples were found, however, of attempts to meet such difficulties. Exceptions were three schools in the survey which produced examples of reports which allowed subject teachers the opportunity to respond differentially.

Reports issued by all three were of the slip type and the individual slips differed for each subject, giving teachers the opportunity to grade performance on a number of subject-specific dimensions and supply comments. In one case a space was available for a comment on each aspect of performance or behaviour which was graded. These reports provided a description of student performance closely tied to specific subject objectives and therefore also produced varying report content across the different year groups. In one school this form of reporting was used in the first two years (students aged 11 to 13) only, with a conventional report book being used thereafter. In the other two schools the approach was retained for the full period of statutory education. One of the schools also provided parents with a description of the aims of each course, thus giving information in an area in which, as had become apparent in Chapter 7, many parents consider themselves particularly ill informed (see Appendix B6). These, together with several initiatives in leavers' reports (see pp. 131—3), were the nearest approaches to what is now commonly described as profile reporting which the project discovered. Such approaches had at the time of our inquiry been supported by funded developmental work in Scotland (SCRE, 1977) and subsequent work carried out by the Schools Council supported our findings concerning the rarity of profiling approaches offering systematic assessments in schools in England and Wales (Balogh, 1982).

iii. Innovations in report types

From modifications to existing report types and developments geared to the needs of special groups of pupils or different subjects we move on to consider more innovatory practices, where a different *type* of report was being used.

INTERIM REPORTS

A number of examples of interim reports were supplied to the project. Such reports offered minimal descriptive comment and concentrated on marks and grades although occasionally an assessment of personal qualities was included. Many of the examples closely resembled the 'grade cards' produced in such large numbers in schools in America and other European countries.

Reasons given for the introduction were first, that in schools where three full reports had formerly been offered to parents they provided basic information while easing the reporting burden on teachers. Second, in other schools which had previously completed a single annual report for each student they were seen as 'improving the service' without, again, unduly or unacceptably adding to the teacher's workload. Many carried an indication of their interim nature, such as:

This is meant to be a brief progress check in between annual reports. This report should be compared with the last report.

This grade card is intended to give you a guide to your child's progress. Since it is necessarily brief it cannot present the full picture given by the normal school report. If you have any queries concerning your child's work please write to the Head of House.

In some cases the interim nature of the report was indicated by the type of assessment information, this being related to progress since the last annual report (e.g. 'Improved', 'Maintained' or 'Poor'). In most cases, however, the achievement and effort grade structure of the full report was retained and only the comments section omitted.

Three schools had novel formats. The first of these consisted of a page which could readily be separated in two. The first section contained ability grades, indications of 'cause for concern' and 'cause for praise' and was added to the school record system. The second section was different in format and offered grades for 'performance', 'effort in class' and 'effort in homework' and was sent home to parents.

The second example carried two items of coded information from each subject teacher, using the following framework:

The letters A to X opposite each subject stand for the features of each pupil's work and behaviour which teachers feel deserve most comment.

The number after each letter compares your child's achievement, attitude or effort with his or her own past performance, not with the performance of other pupils.

1 = Strong   2 = Satisfactory   3 = Needs special attention

A Self reliance.
B Cooperation with other pupils
C Participation in extra activities.
D Effort in oral class work (or PE).
E Effort in written classwork.
F Effort in homework.
G Presentation of work (or PE kit).
H Oral expression.
J Grammar, punctuation and spelling.

K Listening skills.
L Written expression.
M Drawing skills.
N Number skills.
P Practical skills.
Q Observation of evidence (comprehension).
R Forming conclusions (interpretation).
S Memory.
T Using conclusions (judgment).
U Imagination and originality.
V Pronunciation.

X Meeting with parents required.

Parents could indicate their wish to discuss the report's content with teachers and the card was then returned to the school and added to the pupil records.

The third school provided what was termed a 'profile assessment'. Each subject teacher completed a slip offering grading alternatives from 'Always' to 'Very rarely' (five-point scale) for the following:

Classwork: Attentiveness – concentrates on work.
Presentation – work tidy and well laid out.
Participation – joins in class discussion, answers questions, etc.
Homework: Written – done regularly and on time – well presented.
Review – learns and revises each week (based on tests).

The following aspect was headed *'General'* and was graded from 'Very near' to 'Very far off' (five-point scale):

Effort – how close he/she comes to his/her own highest level.

A final section:

Standard reached – with respect to rest of year group (or external examination standard in years 4 and 5)

was graded from 'Very high' to 'Very low', again using a five-point scale.

In most schools, grade cards had to be signed by parents and returned, although one example on NCR paper was submitted. Only one instance of a grade card used for repeated reporting was found and this provided space for a subject achievement grade in October, December, February, Easter and at the spring Bank holiday.

ORAL REPORTING
While many schools supplemented their written reports to parents with oral reporting, a very few used the oral report as their principal means of reporting. Some of these schools were large comprehensive schools with long experience in this approach – extending in some cases over ten years.

Parents, it seems, liked oral reporting and the schools drew attention to the high attendance at parents' evenings. Attendance figures seldom dropped below 90 per cent for any year group, figures that were substantiated by several of the schools over three or four recent years. Most of the schools provided follow-up home visits to ensure contact with parents with whom it was considered essential to discuss progress and some of the schools provided a written copy of the report where parents requested this. This was usually based upon the internal report which provided the framework for the oral report. Heads were concerned to point out, however, that even where such written reports were made available, discussion with staff provided the 'real means of communication'.

Two practices appeared to be consistently associated with oral reporting. First, schools tended to reject the more usual grading policies and a somewhat smaller number recorded a commitment to the encouragement of student attendance at parent—teacher discussions.

Heads emphasized the need to prepare material for the interview and to prepare staff in skills which were not commonly part of their training. One head offered the following observations:

1. The school must   (i) be *convinced* in the first instance that it is viable, useful and beneficial to (a) the school, (b) to parents and (c) to students.

    (ii) examine *critically* how it will affect the school's existing pastoral/reporting system. Will overhaul of existing practices/policies be required?

    (iii) be prepared to accept parents' choice of interview times — can staff stand the inconvenience this may cause?

    (iv) *recognise* this as an essential part of the school's pastoral policy.
2. Meticulous preparatory administrative planning and follow-up is required. At least 4—6 weeks are needed to cover preparation, the interview itself, the follow-up.
3. An agreed check-list is essential for all interviewing teams (e.g. attendance, behaviour, achievements, relationships with students/ teachers/non-teaching staff, academic progress).
4. Staff induction and training for interviewing teams must take place at all levels of the 'hierarchy' from probationers upwards.
5. There must be balance at the interview. Students and parents must not be overwhelmed by numbers in interviewing team.
6. Interviewing techniques must be developed by staff. (It's not Judgement Day!)
7. The provision of comfortable, attractive rooms for interviews (including the Headmaster's office!)

In the light of the difficulties some teachers experienced in discussing pupils' progress with parents, these guidelines might also be appropriate for the more usual parent—teacher discussions following the production of written reports.

Several schools emphasized the part played in school—home relations by open evenings in which displays of work could be shown. These were seen as meeting parents' needs for information concerning their child's work, providing evidence for the comparative assessment of a pupil's performance and leading to useful discussion about the work of the school and the achievements of the individual student.

In one 9—13 middle school, this practice had been developed to provide the means of reporting to parents. The system consisted of the accumulation of a folder of work, each item of which was used as the basis for a discussion involving parent, student and teacher. The system was essentially an oral one, supplemented by the evidence supplied by the work folder. Parents not attending the discussions were visited by the head.

Parent comments made on reply slips attached to the folders of work were scrutinized and interviews with members of staff and pupils conducted. While no evidence could be found to suggest that any of the participants had serious objections to the system, a number of points gave rise to concern. The most important of these related to the method by which the work folder was built up. Since it necessarily involved a strong commitment to presentation rather than content, this resulted in much copying and recopying of individual items of work. Students recorded little conversation with teachers about their work folder and those interviewed had little idea of the way in which their work was being marked. A further area for concern was the nature of teacher comment and parents' response to the work produced. Both seemed brief and general rather than individual and specific, as might have been expected. A third point concerned the exclusive concentration upon written work which resulted from this approach. Student work products which could not be fitted easily into the term folder were necessarily excluded from consideration. Since parents' knowledge of the curriculum was founded on the folder of work, whole areas of the curriculum were thus excluded from the processes of scrutiny and parental involvement. In short, it seems that while there are clearly benefits to be derived from parents being able to see and discuss samples of their child's work together with that of others, steps are needed to avoid some of the difficulties noted in this example.

SCHOOL JOURNALS AND DAILY DIARIES

A number of heads and teachers emphasized that effective communication and reporting needed to be continuous and two-way. Many
French schools use what is called the *'Carnet de Correspondence'*
to bring this about and some half dozen schools in the survey were
using a similar system. Some had slightly modified the conventional
'homework diaries' in use in many schools while others had developed
a more distinctive instrument of their own to allow daily contact
between the school and the home.

One large urban comprehensive school placed the school journal at
the centre of its reporting activity. The journal had been introduced
some five years previously with the approval of the staff, to provide
a daily link between home and school. The head teacher actively
promoted the system: 'I make a fetish about being a front-line head —
getting into the classroom and looking at journals.' Students were
seen as liking their 'passports' although the constant checking, built
into many aspects of school life, which had followed the introduction
of a 'permission section' in which staff had to provide written permission
for any untimetabled activity, resulted in many of the pupils calling
their journal 'The Gestapo Handbook' or 'The Colditz Book'.

The pupils interviewed noted that much of the information produced
by the journal was critical and an inspection of completed journals
confirmed this. A number of younger pupils had found the journal
an effective way of obtaining parental help with homework and although
some of the first-year pupils felt that the journals resulted in some
victimization — particularly of those who were trying desperately to
reform — they wished to retain the system. By the second and third
years pupils were expressing the opinion that they should be 'more
trusted' although they still welcomed the structure, particularly the
reminders to complete homework. Whether such a structure was
conducive to the acquisition of routine (as was claimed) was more
open to question as in use it more closely resembled a prop rather
than a means of developing self-reliance.

Staff felt that the permission section was good for discipline since
it was possible to tell where a pupil ought to be at any point in the
school day by reference to the journal. While teachers on the whole
approved of the system and the change that it had effected in the
school by eliminating the view that 'pastoral care was a disciplinary
dustbin', some recorded doubts concerning the effect that it had on
the work of the form tutor: 'You do tend to get involved in trivial

things and miss out on talking to the kids', and others found the exercise time-consuming and were disappointed by the 'minor information' which dominated the content. Senior teachers with responsibility for overseeing staff mentioned that the journals provided a useful means of monitoring teacher performance, particularly in the area of setting homework.

A valuable attribute identified by some staff was the specificity of the material which was contrasted with the more general information conveyed in the conventional written school report. Other staff, however, thought the material provided by the journal compared unfavourably with the 'clear overview' obtained from the more traditional report. Parents were required to look at the journal daily and sign it, writing notes to teachers where necessary. According to the students interviewed, parents did not appear to make much use of the journal and many described parents' resentment at having to sign it daily — a task usually allocated to mum just before the child left for school.

In another school using the same system but requiring parental responses at half-termly intervals, the head teacher recorded that the journal was used 'extensively for routine notes' although 'lengthy or confidential' messages were invited to be sent through the post. The 'great majority of parents welcomed the day to day record . . . and there was no difficulty in obtaining parental signatures twice termly'.

Similar diaries were also observed in special schools where, as well as carrying information concerning progress and aspects of work with which parents could help, the daily contact was used to monitor medication and therapy. Even in those schools where the nature of the disability might be considered to rule out the safe carriage of a daily diary between the home and the school, the system was seen to be working with considerable success. The major problem appeared to be the organization of the teaching day to allow sufficient time for the teacher to complete the diary entries.

COMPUTER-ASSISTED REPORTING

In the United States and some European countries, notably West Germany, computers are used to assist teachers in their production of reports. Computers frequently provide summative grades and grade point averages and are also involved in the provision of grade cards

Figure 8.2:   *A computer-produced report*

EDUCATION AUTHORITY
****
COMPREHENSIVE SCHOOL
****

HEADMASTER
****

REPORT FOR YEAR ENDING JULY 21ST 1978   NAME ******   FORM ******
****

Subject	Year Mark	Exam Mark	Posn in Set	Comment	Teacher
ENGLISH	68	61	06/29 Set —	A good examination result. Has tried very hard this year.	Mrs
WELSH	65	58	01/32 Set 03	A fairly good examination result. Has made encouraging progress this year.	Mrs
FRENCH	68	61	04/29 Set —	A good examination result. Has worked adequately through the year.	Mrs
HISTORY	40	76	06/31 Set 01	A very good examination result. Always works well. Shows much promise.	Mrs
GEOGRAPHY	51	59	02/29 Set —	A good examination result. Needs constant perseverance in class and homework.	Mrs
REL. INSTRUCTION	43	52	08/29 Set —	A rather poor examination result. Needs constant perseverance in class and homework.	Mrs

Subject				Comment	Teacher
PHYSICS	84	56	10/29 Set —	A good examination result. Has worked well through the year.	Mr
CHEMISTRY	55	49	06/29 Set 03	A fair examination result. Has shown much promise this year.	Mr
BIOLOGY	53	59	08/29 Set —	A good examination result. Has worked adequately through the year.	Mrs
MATHEMATICS	67	58	17/34 Set 01	A fair examination result. Has progressed satisfactorily this year.	Mr
ART	50	58	06/29 Set —	A good examination result. Has made encouraging progress this year.	Mr
MUSIC	60	91	01/29 Set 03	An excellent examination result. Always works well. Shows much promise.	Miss
BOYS' PRACTICAL	62	74	01/16 Set —	An excellent examination result. Always works well. Shows much promise.	Mr
P.E.	52	—	—/— Set —	Fair. Has shown a keen interest this year.	Mr

REMARKS:
****

CONDUCT:
****

ATTENDANCE   POSSIBLE 397   ACTUAL

Form Teacher: Mrs   Head of School: Mrs

Schools' Computer Centre

for parents. In a few cases they are used to assist in the production of a more rounded report.

One school, which provided a computer-printed report (Fig. 8.1) similar in layout and content to a conventional single sheet report, was visited in the course of the project. The computer report had been in use as the end-of-year report in years one, two and three since 1977. As well as entering codes for student, subject, set, position in set, year and examination marks, teachers were asked to select two comments, one covering the examination result and one dealing with the year's work. The comment codes were originated by teaching staff with the assistance of staff from a local-authority-funded schools computer centre. Later modifications in response to staff requests had somewhat reduced the number of alternative comments. No link between a particular mark and a comment was built into the system and, in the event of no suitable comment being available, subject teachers could write in a more apposite phrase of their own. In the summer-term round of reports observed by the team, 44 of the 56 teachers in the school used codes from the two ranges provided, seven used a combination of one pre-selected code and one handwritten comment and five members of staff wrote their own comments. 'Pastoral comments' from the form tutor were always personally written.

All processing was done by staff at the computer centre who had carried out in-service training exercises with the teachers to familiarize them with the approach. The centre was able to provide a two-to-three-day 'turn round' time and felt that similar reports could be produced for all schools in the area.

As well as providing reports the computer centre was able to provide year lists in rank order, thus assisting the allocation of students to ability sets for the second and third years. Additional statistics such as standardized scores and individual and group means were also provided but were not included on the report. The head considered that the provision of the information to aid the school organization had probably had a greater effect than the reporting innovation.

Although the head reported that staff were originally apprehensive concerning the introduction of computerized reporting he felt that they now saw the system as time-saving and accepted it. Teachers recorded that it had taken some time to get used to it but that it now presented no problems although many teachers still regarded it as impersonal.

Parents and students were described as accepting the system and attendance at parents' evenings was described as 'very high', with the head estimating that three quarters or more parents attended in the first three years.

Summary and discussion

Many schools have been examining their reporting systems in recent years and, at the beginning of this chapter, it was reported that over half the schools surveyed had reporting systems less than five years old. Only one in eight had retained the same system for ten years or more. The most common change related to the type of report used was a major trend towards the introduction of slip systems in place of the single sheet or the report book. Changes in the system of marking or grading, in the organization of staff responsibilities for reporting, and in the design of reports, were also common. It was apparent that change could be costly, particularly where large stocks of reports had been ordered so as to reduce unit cost. It was also clear that, as with any innovation, staff attitudes were an important factor in the success of any new system. However, again, there are grounds for optimism; despite the economic constraints confronting schools and the many pressures which these in turn have placed on teaching staff, a sizeable proportion (one in five ordinary schools and one in three special schools) were planning developments to their reporting systems in the academic year immediately following the survey.

Some of the examples of change cited in this chapter involve fairly minor modifications designed to tackle problems common to a particular type of report. We saw, for example, how one school had effected modifications to the slip system in order to overcome the lack of continuity which was seen as one of its defects, while others tried to grapple with the problem of excess space which the slip system posed for some teachers who might, through limited contact with the class, have very little to say. Other examples were of schools which were tackling basic problems which underlie all types of report and in this context we focused on different ways of imparting information on assessments, ranging from schools which had rejected grading to those which sought to refine its crudities by extending and defining more carefully the attributes graded. We looked at reports for special groups — induction reports for new entrants, leaver reports, reports for the less able and also for the more academically gifted. In one of the examples which focused on these abler children, and also in the discussion of oral reporting, attention was drawn to the strategies employed to develop staff skills in talking to pupils about their progress and in conducting interviews with parents.

Oral reporting supplanted the written report in very few schools and was classified among the more innovative practices, reported in the third section of the chapter. Also included in this section were interim reports and daily diaries and journals — both attempts to establish more frequent information exchange with parents — and exhibits of students' work. These were aimed at helping parents gain a better understanding of what their children learned and achieved but were associated with a number of problems, including an over-emphasis on the production of examples of written work.

The chapter concluded with an example of a school using computer-assisted reporting, which is almost certain to become more widespread in the near future. Our example indicated first that a computer-produced report could find acceptability with teachers, parents and pupils and, second, that many advantages could be gained by using a computer for processes associated with reporting, such as the ordering and analysis of assessment data.

Chapter Nine

Guidelines for Change

Although teachers would probably rank marking and reporting at the bottom of their list of preferred activities, there may be no other activity that has greater potential for interpreting the school program, for securing cooperation between home and school, and for promoting development. Despite many years of experimentation and research, the problems and issues related to marking and reporting remain unsettled.

'Marking and reporting pupils' progress', NEA, 1970.

In several places in this report findings have been described as 'encouraging'; we have indeed found evidence for the potential of the report to which the major American study quoted above refers. We have found, too, considerable evidence of schools' readiness to seek ways of improving their reporting systems and in the last chapter some of the more innovatory practices were reviewed. Since the project completed its data collection there has been a growing emphasis on issues surrounding schools' accountability, an increasing awareness of the rights of parents to information concerning their children and a spread in technological innovations which could in time revolutionize report production and the closely related areas of assessment and record-keeping.

This concluding chapter is written primarily for those in schools — heads and their staff — who wish to review and revise their reporting procedures. There are, however, some clear messages for others and in particular for those in LEAs whose task it is to provide professional support for teachers and for those in colleges and departments of education, whether involved in pre- or in-service training. What is attempted in these concluding paragraphs is not a summary — summaries are provided at the end of each chapter — but a synthesis of some major findings in the form of an agenda of issues to consider and questions to ask in schools where review or reform is taking place.

The mechanisms of review and consultation

It was reported in Chapter 2 that heads were almost always closely involved in the selection of their school's reporting system and that usually they were assisted by a staff working party. The sheer volume of work involved in carrying out a serious examination of reporting, together with the need for any proposed revisions to be understood and accepted by staff, clearly suggest a shared approach to the task as being the only one feasible in most cases. While the composition of any working group and its mode of operation will reflect the particular circumstances of the school, our findings suggest that there are groups whose views might be elicited with advantage, either through representation on a working party or by other means. Within schools, these include the following:

(a) Teachers of subjects where assessment and reporting is known to present especial difficulties. In Chapter 5 we noted, for example, that teachers of English, aesthetic and craft subjects cited problems more frequently than other subject teachers, as did teachers of slow learners, and teachers whose contact with pupils was limited.

(b) Probationary teachers, faced with coming to grips with a reporting system which may be unfamiliar to them and for which the chances are they will have received little if any preparation. It was noted in Chapter 4 that probationary teachers were given a similar number of reports to their more experienced colleagues but took substantially longer to complete them.

(c) Teachers with pastoral responsibilities. Our findings call into question the usefulness in their present form to both parents and pupils of the form tutor's report or reports by heads of year and house.

(d) Students. Very little evidence was found of the student body being given an opportunity to express their views concerning reporting, even though they were clearly considered 'consumers' of the report in many instances, and as Chapter 6 indicates, might have much to contribute. Student representation on a working group would be considered inappropriate in many schools, but other strategies for consultation — through tutor systems, subject teachers, school councils and parents' organizations — might be considered.

Outside school, parents are, of course, the major consumers of the school report, but together with school governors, they, too, were rarely consulted about the form the school's reporting should take. In each case only one in ten schools involved them in discussions on the choice of report. Examples of consultative strategies are given in Appendix B4, which illustrates one school's approach to getting parents' views on the importance of certain items of information, and Appendix B7 shows how a head set about involving staff, parents and governors in a review of his school's reporting system. The mechanics of consultation were in some schools undertaken by the parents' association. Active parent association members provide a useful resource although it is important that the consultation process involve as many parents as possible and not only those already most overtly committed to partnership with the school. Although it was not possible within the confines of this study to explore forms of reporting in special schools in any depth, our evidence suggests that there may be a particular need for such schools to ascertain the views and needs of their parents. As was noted in Chapter 2, particular difficulties appeared to be associated with written reports in some special schools and over a quarter did not have them; others, however, were able to employ them in much the same way as ordinary schools.

It was noted in Chapter 2 that heads usually rejected using routine reports to parents as documents for employers. In the last chapter, however, we described how some schools had developed a special report for school leavers and where these are produced, the need for consultation with local employers and the careers service concerning the usefulness of specific items of information is apparent.

A discussion agenda

Working parties generally operate more effectively if they have a clear brief or agenda, and examples of how heads provided this are given in Appendix B7, referred to above, and in Appendix B8, where one head not only sets the task but provides the answers!

This report has suggested a number of critical issues which might appear as items for discussion in any school review:

i.   The function and audience of reports

It was noted in Chapter 2 that the report was seen as fulfilling one or more of the functions of *informing, motivating* and *involving* and that its audience comprised parents, pupils, heads and other teachers. One head who had analysed report content discovered that recently qualified teachers tended to address their comments to their head of department rather than to parent or pupil. Here, and in other schools, heads feared that the language used by many teachers was inappropriate, using educational jargon unfamiliar to parents and failing to give an indication of how faults might be remedied.

Critical questions here, then, are 'Who is the report for?' and 'What is it intended to achieve?'

ii.   The report in the context of other school records

It was apparent from Chapter 3 that the report was but one of a number of records kept by schools on individual pupils. While heads considered that reports made major contributions to the academic, pastoral and careers work in their schools, it was noted that on a wide range of issues, other internal records were used more frequently in staff discussions on individual pupils. Questions were posed in Chapter 3 concerning the extent to which the report to parents duplicates or complements other school records and what information is routinely recorded on pupils and not made available to parents, and why. Such questions are clearly pertinent in any school's scrutiny of its reporting and record-keeping procedures.

iii.   The content of the report

The majority of heads were agreed that comments on achievement, progress, effort and attitude, together with grades for achievement and effort in each subject, pastoral comment, and items such as attendance and lateness totals and a record of extra-curricular activities should appear on the report. They were equally agreed in rejecting the inclusion of the student's position in class or in individual subjects and student comment similarly met with little enthusiasm. We noted in Chapter 2 that a number of items which heads considered important had no headed space on the report forms and might consequently be overlooked unless teachers were carefully briefed as to their inclusion and appropriate checks carried out. Any review of a reporting procedure might profitably include consideration of the report layout, how it is used by teachers, and the values and emphases which it transmits to parents.

The evidence of both parents and pupils (Chapters 6 and 7) poses some further questions relating to content. The first concerns if and how the report can be made more useful in giving parents and students information which will help in making educational and vocational decisions. In particular, some indication was required of likely performance in public examinations and it is here, perhaps, that we find one of the most problematic areas. Teachers' concern about giving information which might demotivate was apparent and in the detailed analysis of grades on reports over three years reported in Chapter 5, it was noted that while their grading became progressively more severe as public examinations drew near, it was still consistently generous in terms of the results their students obtained. There is some evidence, too, of a conflict in what both parents and students claimed to want; both preferred that the student's work be compared with his or her previous performance rather than with others in the same class or age group. Yet such ipsative assessment is clearly incompatible with assessment predictive of external examination performance. Our evidence suggests a need for examination by teachers, parents and pupils of the kinds of information that are needed to help older pupils with the decisions that confront them and the place of the report in making such information available.

It is apparent from the preceding discussion that it is impossible to consider the content of the report without considering the assessment procedures which a school operates. In Chapter 5 heads' and teachers' perceptions of some of the problems associated with grading were recorded, and it was noted that in a substantial number of schools teachers were attempting to construct grades on the basis of conflicting criteria. It may be that schools planning a review of their reporting procedures find it necessary to carry out a parallel examination of their grading and assessment policies and how these are applied in different subject disciplines. Our findings point to the necessity of ensuring that any grading policy is fully understood by the teachers who have to implement it and that parents understand what the grades on their child's report mean. One in three parents studied felt that the information given on the school's grading policy was inadequate and a similar proportion did not know the basis on which grades were allocated (Chapter 7). A full and clear description of what the grades mean must form a crucial element in the content of any report.

One of the most forceful pleas to come from both parents and pupils was for more detailed information and advice. Parents wanted to know what their child had been doing and pupils expressed a need for detailed comment on work recently completed. It was noted in the case study of student self-assessment that they tended to focus on detail in accounts of their progress and it seems that the balanced generalized overview which teachers sometimes strive for in commenting on a pupil's performance is little valued by parent or pupil. It may be for this reason that the comments of form or year tutors were not held in great esteem, although this was not the case when the form tutor made a substantial contribution to the report, as in the example cited in Chapter 7, where he completed a slip giving a fairly extensive review of the pupils' progress.

iv. The choice of format

The predominance of two types of report, the single sheet and the report slip, was noted, with slips being more commonly employed with older pupils and in schools where the system of reporting had undergone change in the last five years. Slip reports require longer to complete and also involve considerable time to collate; indeed, examples of schools occurred which had experimented with a slip system but later rejected it because of the extra burden it imposed on staff. This must be balanced by the large number of schools which had adopted it because it offered flexibility, the opportunity for more extensive comment, and avoided such dangers as the halo effect and the problems which arose when staff had to queue for a single sheet report. There was some evidence, too, that parents favoured a slip system.

Some of the examples of more innovatory practice described in the last chapter suggest some questions which schools grappling with the problem of which types of report to opt for might consider. Is there a place for a briefer interim report or indeed for some form of daily journal as was adopted by one school in the study? What is the place of oral reporting and when can it be used to supplement or even supplant the written report? Do school leavers require a different kind of report, which can serve a dual audience of parents and employers? Should there be a special form of 'settling-in' report for pupils in the intake year and those who join the school subsequently?

v. The timing of reports and the organization of the reporting procedure

Very few schools (five per cent) in fact provided a settling-in report (Chapter 3) and, indeed, under half issued any form of written report in the first term. While many schools made reports available at important choice points — for example in the spring term of the third, fifth, sixth and seventh years — the data confirm the long established practice of issuing students with reports at the end of the summer term. In Chapter 3 we questioned the wisdom of this practice from two angles. First, in terms of improving students' motivation such timing is unlikely to be effective simply because any resolutions formed must be sustained over the summer vacation and the teachers and courses encountered after it may be different. Second, in terms of teacher workload, it gives rise to considerable pressure at one point in the academic year. Our study of the length of time teachers took to complete a set of reports produced the unsurprising but nonetheless important finding that the more reports teachers had to complete, the less time they spent on each. Many schools have already recognized the advantages in staggering the reporting load throughout the year.

In Chapter 4 it was noted that the average time for a subject report was nearly six minutes and for a report giving the tutor's overview, nearly ten. We pointed out that while this does not seem long to report on what may be a year's work, writing a report may be regarded as the tip of the iceberg, being sustained by the far more extensive activities of assessment and recording throughout the year. Some teachers noted the time that could be saved at the report-writing stage if proper records were kept and it was possible to base a comment or grade on a careful overview of records of pupils' performance throughout the year. Examination of how teachers' record-keeping systems can be adapted to facilitate the reporting process might prove a fruitful area of study for a school reviewing its reports.

One part of the reporting process which clearly took up a great deal of time in many schools was that of checking reports. Checks, double checks and sometimes treble checks were carried out, with heads, most of whom were happy to delegate the organizational aspects of reporting, frequently coming in at this last stage before the report finally left the school. This, of course, testifies to the importance which heads attach to the report; it also suggests that there may be considerable duplication of effort unless each checker is briefed to scrutinize distinct aspects.

vi.   In-service needs related to reporting

Generally, teachers receive no preparation in either initial or in-service training for reporting, and in Chapter 5 it was noted that fewer than one in three had received any training in related areas such as assessment. The LEA contribution in this area was sparse, with very few examples of LEAs having offered advice or support to schools as to how they might tackle reporting to parents. Schools were therefore forced to develop their own policies and guidelines and three quarters had some form of written guidance for their teachers.

Two areas are suggested by this study as those where secondary teachers particularly require support. The first, relating to assessment techniques and strategies, is by now fairly widely acknowledged (see, for example, DES, 1979). The second concerns helping teachers to develop their skills in the parent interview. Talking to parents about their child's progress, behaviour and possible educational and vocational future is a task with inbuilt hazards. Both teachers and parents in this study valued the contacts they had with each other, but teachers recorded a need for some preparation in this part of their work. In the last chapter an example was given of a school where oral reporting was seen to involve particular preparation and skills and systematic steps had been taken to give teachers the confidence necessary to cope with parental discussion.

Schools considering the in-service implications of any developments in their reporting procedures will have to consider possible sources of support and assistance. Some schools may have within their own teaching community staff who are particularly experienced or gifted in areas such as parental interviewing, or with specialist knowledge of assessment and statistical techniques, which they can share with their colleagues if the time can be organized for them to do so. The possible resource afforded by neighbouring schools who may face similar difficulties also merits attention, and LEA advisory services may prove a valuable source of information on the variety of local practice, as well as having, with teachers' centres and colleges, a key role as providers of in-service courses and activities which might develop teachers' reporting skills.

vii. The parental response to the report

In Chapter 7 we looked at the two main methods schools use to elicit a response to the report from parents. The written reply slip, which many schools use and more are seeking to introduce, appears to have a disappointingly low take-up by parents; it was noted, however, in Chapter 7 that this method had considerable potential as a means of home—school dialogue and in Chapter 8, examples were given of strategies which schools employed to increase the number of parents using reply slips. The second method, the parents' evening following the issue of the report, was also widely used and it was noted that while these occasions were generally valued by parents and teachers alike, aspects of their administration provoked criticism from parents (but rarely received comment from teachers). In particular, parents commented on having to queue for substantial periods of time for a few minutes' talk with a teacher, and many schools had introduced appointments systems to avoid this difficulty. Less susceptible of resolution is the lack of privacy in which discussions with parents take place, although, again, examples were found of schools demonstrating considerable ingenuity in the deployment of the space available to provide suitable interviewing areas.

One of the most important challenges to schools which emerges from this study concerns how to capitalize on parents' positive reactions to the report. Parents saw the report as useful and almost half of them thought that it would change their child's way of working at school; some intended to modify their own behaviour in terms of providing supervision, encouragement and better facilities for study. What parents very often lacked, however, was any guidance as to exactly *how* they could help their child to do better. As already noted, they were often critical of vague and unspecified exhortations to improvement, and it seems that a question which any school review group might consider is what exactly the school expects parents to *do* once the report is received.

viii. *The student response*

A finding which emerges clearly from the evidence and which deserves underlining in these concluding remarks is that the report *matters* to students. Nearly all find in it some useful information and it is widely discussed with friends, as well as parents. Both 'good' and 'bad' reports stimulate the intention to change and work harder and the question arises, as with parents, as to how schools can capitalize on the initial positive reactions which the report produces.

An evident problem here concerns teachers' scepticism. Teachers were generally dismissive of the report's effectiveness in promoting behavioural change, and considered that any effects were short-lived. Such perceptions may well be correct; indeed, given what appears to happen from the pupils' viewpoint following the receipt of the report, it would be surprising if they were not. We have already noted that students, like their parents, felt the need for specific advice concerning how they could improve their performance. Without this, initial good intentions may well dissipate, simply through lack of direction. Over half the students in this study had not discussed their report with *any* of their teachers and 40 per cent of the subject teachers and pastoral tutors had not, for their part, discussed reports with *any* of their students. Clearly, teachers in their day-to-day contacts with students are constantly discussing progress and it may seem that specific discussion of the comment on the report is unnecessary. Such a view fails, however, to take account both of the opportunity which the report affords to take advantage of students' resolutions, and also of the clearly expressed desires of both students and parents for detailed guidance on the courses of action to adopt to bring about improvement.

We concluded in Chapter 6 that it was important for schools to find ways of making time available for teachers to discuss reports with students, so that students and teachers can select which aspects of the student's work merit particular attention and effort, and work out a plan of campaign together. We also reported, however, that time was not the only factor that appeared to be associated with staff—student discussion and that more experienced teachers were more likely to discuss reports with their students. The kind of counselling and guidance skills which such discussions require are too rarely recognized, the assumption being that all teachers possess them, even though there is generally little in their training which would suggest they should. Critical questions, then, for any school working party on reports to consider concern how to capitalize on students' initial good intentions. How can the report best be followed up with both students and parents; how can time be organized for such follow-up; and what training and support will staff require for these developments in the reporting process?

To this agenda, schools will wish to add their own items, arising from this study or from their own particular experiences. What is clear is that any thorough review of reporting will involve considerable commitment, focusing on the central aspects of the school's activity and the relationships encompassed by it. Because of this, it is likely to have spin-offs in many areas besides the report to parents and may involve re-assessing fundamental policies and practices along the way. Also likely is that such a review will not seek to produce a 'once and for all' solution, but will recognize first, that the report may require adaptation to reflect developments in the school's organization and curriculum and, second, that since reporting is above all about communicating, it can only usefully be regarded as a changing and dynamic activity.

Appendix A

Tables referred to in text

Table A1
(a) The respondent sample — by school type

School type	*Population†* (England & Wales) N	%			*Respondents* N	%	*Response rate* %
Middle/secondary	564	11			106	14	—
Secondary modern	837	17			101	14	—
Grammar	407	8			38	5	—
Technical and other	97	2			21	3	—
Comprehensive	3,083	62			474	64	—
Totals:			*Sample*				
Ordinary schools	4,988	100	945††	(19%)	740	100	78.3
Special schools	1,541		152	(10%)	97	—	63.8
				Overall response rate			76.3

† Source: *Statistics of Education*, **1**, HMSO, 1977.
†† Approximately one per cent of the schools had ceased to exist by the time the sample was approached.

(b) Special schools

Provision	Population† (N = 1,541) %	Respondents (N = 97) %
ESN(M)	34	26
ESN(S)	27	38
ESN(M) and (S)	2	3
Maladjusted	11	11
Physically handicapped	5	4
Delicate	3	1
Physically handicapped and delicate	4	3
Partially sighted	1	1
Epileptic	1	2
Autistic	1	2
Multiple disability	1	1
Hospital	10	2
All other	1	6
Totals	100	100

† Source: *Statistics of Education*, 1, HMSO, 1977.

Table A2
(a) Respondent sample — by school size

Number of pupils	Population (England & Wales) Secondary and middle/secondary† N	%	Respondents N	%
0 — 300	279	5	33	4
301 — 400	366	7	47	6
401 — 600	1,077	22	145	20
601 — 800	1,025	21	120	16
801 — 1,000	790	16	131	18
1,001 — 1,500	1,178	24	213	29
1,501 and more	274	5	51	7
Totals	4,988	100	740	100

† Source: *Statistics of Education*, 1, HMSO, 1977.

(b) Special schools

Number of pupils	Schools	
	N	%
0 − 50	21	26
51 − 100	37	45
101 − 150	16	20
151 +	8	10
Totals	82†	101††

† Unknown size: 15.
†† Rounding error.

Table A3: Teachers' experience in full-time teaching

Years in full-time teaching	Teachers†	
	N	%
Probationers (less than 1 year)	31	5
1 − 3 years	83	13
4 − 6 years	109	17
7 − 10 years	132	21
11 − 15 years	107	17
16 − 20 years	62	10
More than 20 years	110	17
Totals	634	100

† N = 647; non-respondents: 13.

Table A4: The characteristics of the schools in the parent and pupil surveys

School	Size/ age range	Catchment	Organization by year	Reporting system
A	879 11–16 years Mixed	Mixed housing in an urban setting with elements of deprivation. Restricted catchment area	1⎫ 2⎬Mixed ability 3⎭ 4⎱Option groups 5⎰	An annual slip report issued over all three terms
B	790 11–18 years Mixed	Being renovated. Urban council estate. Isolated from city. Restricted catchment area	1⎫ 2⎬Mixed ability 3⎭ 4⎱Option groups 5⎰	Two sheets issued to all years at the same time
C	809 11–16 years Mixed	New council estate at city edge; rural fringe with poor public transport	1⎱ Mixed ability 2⎰ Mixed ability 3 and sets 4⎱Option groups 5⎰	One slip issued over two terms. One slip issued at end of year to all year groups.
D	808 11–16 years Mixed	Established 'new town' and extensive rural area with poor public transport	1⎱Mixed ability 2⎰ 3 Banded 4⎱Option groups 5⎰	One sheet issued over two terms, one sheet at end of summer
E	1,688 11–18 years Mixed	Owner-occupied housing at edge of 'county town'; large rural area with poor transport	1 Banded 2⎱Ability sets 3⎰ 4⎱Option groups 5⎰	Two sheets and one book each year, all issued at same time
F	1,421 11–18 years Mixed	Small town with rural catchment; poor public transport	1⎱Sets, bands and 2⎰mixed ability 3 Streamed 4⎱Option groups 5⎰	Two slips each year all issued at same time. Parents collect reports

Table A5: Head teacher opinions of the value of including selected items on the report

Nature of item	% of head teachers (N = 740)						
	Essential to include	Of moderate value	Uncertain	Of little value	Should not appear	Non-response	Totals
Attendance total	67	17	3	8	4	2	101†
Comment on attendance	49	35	6	5	1	5	101†
Lateness total	47	26	8	10	4	5	100
Punctuality comment	45	37	6	6	2	5	101†
Class position	6	11	8	20	52	4	101†
Subject position	15	21	7	15	39	4	101†
Examination position	15	23	7	15	35	4	99†
Subject comment	96	2	—	1	—	1	100
Pastoral comment	91	6	1	—	—	2	100
Summary of subject reports	57	22	8	7	2	5	101†
Effort grade	69	12	5	6	5	3	100
Comment on effort	80	13	2	1	1	3	100
Attitude grade	35	16	14	13	15	8	101†
Comment on attitude	73	16	4	1	1	4	99†
Behaviour/conduct grade	23	11	15	17	25	9	100
Comment on behaviour	75	17	3	1	1	3	100
Attainment grade	68	13	5	4	4	6	100
Comment on attainment	83	12	1	1	1	3	101†

Personal development grade	11	15	20	16	30	8	100
Comment on personal development	51	27	12	2	3	5	100
Examination grade	55	22	7	5	5	6	100
Homework grade	12	25	19	18	16	10	100
Homework comment	49	34	8	3	2	5	101†
Progress grade	22	17	19	14	18	10	100
Comment on progress	76	14	4	1	1	5	101†
GCE/CSE predictive grade	24	23	15	5	20	14	101†
Commendations/merits	41	25	11	8	9	7	101†
Demerits	12	20	17	18	26	8	101†
Comment by student	2	9	36	11	33	10	101†
Space for comment by parents	51	24	14	3	5	4	101†
Extra-curricular activity	60	32	4	1	1	3	101†

† Rounding error.

Table A6: The annual number of reports issued shown by year group
(a) Ordinary schools

Number of reports each year	% of schools with pupils in year group						
	Year 1 (N=605)	Year 2 (N=653)	Year 3 (N=622)	Year 4 (N=601)	Year 5 (N=594)	Year 6 (N=380)	Year 7 (N=368)
1	37	38	38	34	65	33	65
2	57	57	56	60	32	63	33
3	5	5	5	6	2	3	1
4	—	—	—	—	1	—	—
5	—	—	—	1	—	1	—
6	1	1	1	—	—	—	—
Totals	100	101†	100	101†	100	100	99†
Non-respondents	13	9	6	14	21	13	25

† Rounding error.

(b) Special schools

Number of reports each year		% of schools with pupils in year group		
	Year 1 (N=47)	Year 2 (N=45)	Year 3 (N=45)	Year 4 (N=44)	Year 5 (N=42)
1	79	78	79	77	76
2	15	16	16	16	17
3	6	7	7	7	7
Totals	100	100	101†	100	100
Non-respondents	27	25	25	26	28

† Rounding error.

Table A7: Teacher involvement in teaching and reporting as a
main subject

Subject area	Teachers (N = 647†)	
	N	%
Aesthetics and craft	116	18
Commerce/business studies	23	4
English	75	12
Humanities other than English	105	17
Mathematics	79	12
Modern/classical languages	51	8
Physical education	29	5
Remedial education	27	4
Sciences	101	16
Teachers offering more than one main subject	27	4
Totals	633	100

† Missing cases: 14.

Table A8: Teachers' length of service in present school

Years of service	Teachers (N = 647†)	
	N	%
Less than 1 year	67	11
1 — 3 years	152	24
4 — 6 years	174	27
7 — 10 years	131	21
11 — 15 years	48	7
16 — 20 years	39	6
More than 20 years	25	4
Totals	636	100

† Missing cases: 11.

Table A9: The time the current system had been in operation cross-tabulated with the major report types in use in year two† (ordinary and special schools)††

Length of time the reporting system has been in operation	Slip reports	% of schools providing Single sheets	Report books
Less than 1 year	10	7	5
1 − 4 years	56	43	30
5 − 9 years	30	35	33
More than 10 years	4	16	33
Totals	100	101†††	101†††

† Year two is used to illustrate the results since it contained the fewest missing cases. All other year groups produced results significant at the same level.

†† $\chi^2 = 67.10$, $p < .001$. Missing cases (including schools not providing slip, sheet or book reports): 42.

††† Rounding error.

Table A10: Teacher difficulties with grading/reporting main subjects

Subject	Number of teachers†	Number with difficulties	%
Remedial education	27	20	74
English	75	38	51
Aesthetics and craft	116	50	43
Physical education	29	10	34
Modern and classical languages	51	17	33
Humanities other than English	105	26	25
Mathematics	79	12	15
Sciences	101	14	14
Commerce/business studies	23	2	9
Total	633	189	30

† N = 633; non-respondents: 14.

Table A11: Analytic framework for teachers' written comments

Area of comment	Value†	Detail
Ability	+	High ability, good understanding, intelligent
	M	Able in some aspects, less able in others. Of average ability, reasonable grasp, capable
	−	Low ability, poor understanding, finds subject difficult
Attitude	+	Positive attitude, interest, enjoys subject
	M	Moderated interest comment
	−	Negative attitude, no interest
Behaviour	+	Good behaviour, cooperative/pleasant, polite, friendly
	M	Behaviour fluctuates (moderated comment)
	−	Poor behaviour, disruptive/rude/chatting
Confidence	+	Confident
	−	Shy, quiet, nervous, lack of self-confidence
Effort	+	Effort good, concentration high, working hard
	M	Effort inconsistent; average effort
	−	Poor effort, no power of concentration/lazy/idle

Examination results obtained	+	Good examination result
	M	Mediocre exam result, adequate, fair, satisfactory
	–	Poor exam result
Homework	+	Consistently good homework
	M	Moderated comment
	–	Homework poor or absent
Maturity	+	Mature, responsible, serious, reliable, sensible, demonstrates leadership
	M	Sometimes acts maturely; other moderated comments
	–	Immature, irresponsible, childish, silly, easily led
Participation	+	Participation good
	M	Uneven participation
	–	Poor participation
Presentation	+	Neat written work, well presented
	M	Written work variable
	–	Poor presentation, careless, scrappy
Progress	+	Good, considerable progress, excellent
	M	Coping, satisfactory/steady, reasonable
	–	Poor/disappointing

† + indicates positive value; – indicates negative value; and M is used for categories containing both negative and positive comments, or comments indicating an average or middle position. Pastoral comments and comments concerned with remediation were not attributed values.

Table A11: *continued*

Area of comment	*Value†*	*Detail*
Prognostic	+ M —	Could do well Could do moderately well Will not do well
Remediation		Vague/general recommendations Specific recommendations
Administrative	+ —	Attendance excellent/good Poor attendance/lateness. Disregard of uniform
Pastoral comments		Review of subject reports Extra-curricular participation/non-participation

† + indicates positive value; — indicates negative value; and M is used for categories containing both negative and positive comments, or comments indicating an average or middle position. Pastoral comments and comments concerned with remediation were not attributed values.

Appendix B1

Examples of Guidance Provided for Teachers on Assessment and Report Writing

School 1

Extracts from the school's handbook

ASSESSMENT AND RECORD KEEPING
There are four main reasons for assessment and recording:
  i   to help the teacher to help the pupil;
 ii   to provide those who require information about a pupil, both inside and outside the school, with useful knowledge;
iii   to improve a teacher's professional competency in techniques of assessment;
 iv   to enhance a pupil's self-knowledge.

ASSESSMENT
There are various forms of assessment used within this school.
  i   *The assessment of certain skills* by nationally standardised tests, e.g. NFER, VROs, reading ages . . . Such assessment is recorded in the pupil's record.
 ii   *The language of assessment* used in School Reports is important when relevant, meaningful comments are to be made. Parents are influenced by a teacher's comments . . . Form teachers file duplicate copies of reports in the pupil's folder.
iii   *Day-to-day assessment* should be an integral part of the teaching process in any subject and remains within the teacher's own records.
 iv   *Subject assessment*: it is essential that the records of an individual pupil contain a subject assessment in the form of a grade for each year in which the subject has been studied. Each department must

have a clear policy on the criteria and method by which it arrives at its assessment grade is its concern. However, the manner in which it records that decision is the business of the whole school.

Norm-referenced assessment: There are two main systems of recording norm-referenced assessment, the Literal Grading (A–E) and the Standardised Mark System. The Literal Grade System is used in this school. A and E represent 5% of the population at each end of the ability range, B and D the next 25% and C the middle 40%. The norm is the child population of the year-group in the school. These grades are recorded on the *duplicate* copy of the NCR report only.

Criterion-referenced assessment; The norm-referenced assessment is used in the first three years of the school. In the fourth and fifth years criterion-referenced assessment operates. Grades are allocated according to pre-determined levels of performance and without reference to the standards achieved by other pupils. A CSE Grade 1; B – 2/3; C –4; D – 5; E – Ungraded. These grades are also recorded on the *duplicate* report only.

School 2

i. Extract from the advice offered to staff on the introduction of a slip report system

Reports should be positive, giving constructive advice to parents and pupils on how a pupil can improve himself.

As there is more room for comment some of the areas which *could* be commented upon are:
1. Enthusiasm and attitude to the subject
2. Discipline within the class situation
3. General presentation
4. Oral participation
5. Strengths and weaknesses in the subject
6. Ways in which a pupil could help himself
7. Homework

The form tutor's report *could* include comments upon:
(a) Punctuality and attendance
(b) General attitudes
(c) Personality

The form tutor's report is *not* a summary of the subject report and form tutors are advised to complete it *before* they read the subject reports.

The form tutors have a very important job checking on their form's reports for spelling mistakes and any omissions . . .

ii. Extract from follow-up advice to staff after the first issue of slip reports

The following comments are the result of feedback from parents and staff. The majority of the reports were detailed, perceptive and of a very high standard but the following points should be noted.

1. Comments on reports should be constructive with definite advice to parents wherever possible.
2. The Lower VI reports are perhaps the most important reports which will be written about pupils as they will form the basis of UCCA applications and references to industry so please give extra time and thought to these.
3. If a subject is set please draw parents' attention to the fact in your report if it is relevant, e.g. 'A pleasing exam score, John came top of the 3rd set and as a result of his good efforts and progress over the year he is to be moved into set 2.'
4. Form tutors' reports should not be a summary of subject reports but should show knowledge of what the pupil has contributed to the school, house or tutor group. Parents like to be re-assured that their son/daughter is 'a cheerful, polite and ever helpful pupil', it may be the one glimmer of hope in a disappointing report. Quite reasonably the parents expect the tutor's comments to be the most substantial of all.
5. Will staff please complete the attendance as a fraction $\dfrac{\text{actual}}{\text{possible}}$ as well as commenting on punctuality.
6. Subject staff need to complete the grade for effort and achievement as well as adding the exam %.
7. Staff should not pose questions in their reports, e.g. 'Andrew is either lazy or lacking ability.' We are expected in our professional capacity to distinguish between the possibilities.
8. Do not use derogatory statements about pupils, or try to be sarcastic. Instead point to the specific problems that have arisen. 'Ann shows very little interest in this subject. She resents criticism and either

sulks or becomes aggressive instead of trying to understand where she went wrong.' 'John is too often aggressive and occasionally rude. This is usually an attempt to cover up for lack of effort or concentration. He finds it impossible to accept criticism in front of his class mates and when approached on his own simply becomes silent and unco-operative.' 'Alan has continued to demonstrate his immaturity of mind and is not to be trusted in any situation.'

School 3

Extract from Report Information Sheet to teachers

1. The standard of reporting reflects a number of attitudes in the school. It shows:
   (a) The interest of teachers in their pupils.
   (b) The attitude of the teacher towards his/her subject.
   (c) The willingness of the teacher to take trouble to inform the parents of the progress of their child.
   (d) The school's own standards towards accuracy and presentation.
   It is, therefore, very important that this task is undertaken properly. Neatness, accuracy and constructiveness are all-important. Errors must be corrected if they are made and this only adds to the time spent on the job. Please make every effort to complete the task accurately the first time.
2. The slip system has two main advantages:
   (a) The teacher can write the report when he or she feels like it without having to wait for books or report sheets to become available. This may also be a disadvantage in that it is possible to miss out a child. It is, therefore, essential to tick a list in the mark-book each time a child's report is written. If you are not sure of the pupils' names it is often better to write the report with the class in front of you.
   (b) The other advantage is that there is space for a constructive comment on each child without being influenced by previous teachers' comments or by what you wrote last time.
   This again has its disadvantages in that you are expected to make a constructive comment. A VAGUE PLATITUDE WILL NOT BE SUFFICIENT.

3. For the benefit of those who have not reported before, may I comment that in my opinion one can often judge a teacher by the reports they have written.

    For all staff there are certain reports I have found unacceptable in the past:

(a) Those containing errors or slang.

(b) Those that criticise the natural abilities of the pupil. Too often these cannot be altered, e.g. 'John is a stupid boy', or, 'John will never improve because he finds difficulty in holding a pen.'

(c) Those that criticise the parents or other teachers.

(d) Those that attack a part of the school policy. (I would not accept a comment that suggested that a child was failing because he was being withdrawn for extra reading tuition.)

    Comments must show the teacher's understanding of the pupil's problems and point the way to an improvement (or to further improvement).

School 4

Head teacher's guidance circular offered at the beginning of a new report cycle

PLEASE AVOID THE FOLLOWING ERRORS – ALL OF WHICH OCCURRED IN REPORTS LAST TERM

1. *Spelling* (These are the correct versions!)
    receive, achieve, believe (normal rule is 'i' before 'e' except after 'c'), lose (unlike choose) – (loose means free, untied, etc.), thoroughly, disappointing, separate, absence, concentrate, revise, conscientious, definite, (un)necessary, success, independent, exercise, quite (not quiet!), all right (two words!), until, practise (verb), practice (noun), occur – occurred. (Check that girls' names are spelt correctly.)

2. *Punctuation etc.* Apostrophe: Joanna's work has improved
                            Joanna has done a good term's work
    Sentences are not joined together by a comma (or with nothing!)
    e.g. Joanna has worked hard, she should do well in the summer.
          Joanna has worked hard she should do well . . . etc.
    Correct: Joanna has worked hard and should do well etc.
          or Joanna has worked hard; she should do well etc.
          or Joanna has worked hard. She should do well etc.

3. *Style etc.* Use *complete* sentences for your remarks unless you wish to use brief expression only — e.g. Excellent work.

avoid 'catch up on' . . . use 'catch up with'
or 'cover lost ground'

avoid 'improved on' . . . use just 'improved'

avoid 'quite a lot' and 'rather a lot'

'quite' and 'rather' are adverbs (quite good,
rather slow)

'quite a lot of' = much, many

avoid the multitudinous use of 'get'. A more exact verb would be an improvement

4. Very frequent confusion of 'disinterested' with 'uninterested'

'disinterested' means — impartial, without an 'axe to grind' etc.

'uninterested' means — lacking in interest

Joanna is uninterested in her work

     "   lacks interest   "

     "   not interested   "

Note The errors mentioned here are the most frequent and are the ones which I find most irritating. There are others — but these are sufficient for the present!

Appendix B2

Home, school and college: a discussion paper prepared by the Surrey Inspectorate

(Copies obtainable from Media Resources Centre, Glyn House, Ewell, KT17 2AR. Price 50p.)

(a) *Questions concerned with why parents and teachers should work together*

  (i) How far do we achieve any consistency between the expectations of parents and teachers for the children in our school?

 (ii) Is it possible for home and a comprehensive school to be complementary for the majority of children?

(iii) What goals have we as a staff in common with the parents of our children and in what ways may our goals differ?

 (iv) Could we get more support and help for our children's learning from their parents?

  (v) Do we actually know the attitudes of parents over moral and sex education and where we agree and differ? Should we know more about their views on these matters than we do?

 (vi) What does a teacher need to know about the background and experience of the children he teaches?

(vii) What responsibility has the school to keep the parent informed about the child's progress?

(viii) What should a parent monitor about the school his child attends?

 (ix) How high a priority should we give to establishing and maintaining close relationships with parents?

  (x) Do we do anything to discourage parents?

(b) *Questions concerned with the induction of new pupils*

  (i) How do the arrangements we make for getting to know new parents appear from the parents' point of view?

(ii) Do we give new parents enough chance to tell us about their children; to ask questions?

(iii) Would new parents like opportunities to meet and talk with senior pupils? If so, how can this be arranged?

(iv) What do new parents really want to know about the school? Do we provide all they want?

(v) (a) What information should be issued to new or prospective parents?

    (b) Is there a place for a handbook for new pupils, or for the pupils and their parents?

(c) *Questions concerned with reporting to parents*

(i) What do parents and pupils need to know about courses at the end of the second year, if they are to make sensible choices for their last two years of compulsory schooling?

(ii) (a) How do our parents regard our system of reports?

    (b) How would we view the prospect of including in the report (where this is not already done)

      (i) Suggestions for helping the child to overcome difficulties

      (ii) Comments on career prospects

      (iii) Space for comment by parents and by pupils

      (iv) A report on the experience and qualifications of teachers

      (v) A space in which teacher or parent could request an interview

    (c) What do we believe is the purpose of written reports?

(iii) What other written communication should we have with parents?

(iv) How sure are we that the communication we have is effective? How many parents actually read and take in what we send out? Could we make it more effective?

(d) *Questions concerned with personal contact with parents*

(i) What kinds of events are most useful in actually getting to know parents?

(ii) How well do our parents understand our pastoral structure? Do they always ask to see the head?

(iii) Which teachers should a child's parents meet?

(iv) What preparation should a teacher make for meeting parents for individual discussion?

(v) What training does a teacher need in order to deal adequately with parents? Can we provide it?

(vi) Do we keep adequate records of discussions with parents?

(vii) How many parents of the children for whom he has pastoral responsibility, can each teacher recognize by name? Should we aim to know them all between us?

(viii) What actually happens to a parent who calls at the school without an appointment? What happens to the parent who rings up?

(e) *Questions concerning parent attendance*

(i) Are any of our parents put off by anything in our school?

(ii) Do we do enough to welcome those parents who find school intimidating?

(iii) Do we make those parents who come feel that they are important to us?

(iv) Do we accept too easily the idea that some parents are just not interested? (A number of studies show such parents to be a very small minority.)

(v) Do we cater for a wide enough range of parental interest in activities?

(vi) Are we sure that invitations reach parents?

(f) *A further series of statements were made about the quality of parent—teacher relations in school and teachers were asked to pose the question 'Is this true in our school?'*

(i) Parents know what the school is aiming at and how the teachers are setting out to achieve it.

(ii) Every effort is made to involve parents as soon as their child joins the school.

(iii) Every parent is known to at least one teacher in the school.

(iv) Parents have many opportunities to make judgments about the standards of learning, teaching and the content in all subjects.

(v) Parents understand the pastoral and academic structure of the school and know how to use it.

(vi) All parents feel welcome in the school and are treated as partners in the education of their children.

(vii) Parents are kept fully informed about their child's progress, potential and achievement.

(viii) All parents have regular and adequate opportunities to talk over their children's progress and any difficulties they are encountering, with teachers who know the children well.

(ix) Teachers listen to and take note of parents' views of their children's progress and the school is aware of each parent's views about his child.

(x) Parents are made to feel that they have a contribution to make to their children's education which is recognized and appreciated by the school.

(xi) Parents feel supported, rather than intimidated by the professional expertise of teachers, and this helps them in bringing up their children.

(xii) Parents know a great deal about the courses which are offered to their children when they are asked to make choices and are aware of the implications of these choices for future employment.

(xiii) All teachers prepare adequately for meetings with parents and make notes of important points from these meetings.

(xiv) Inexperienced teachers are trained for their work with parents and supported in it until they are competent.

(xv) The school uses every kind of parent skill to enrich the curriculum.

(xvi) There are parent/teacher activities to suit all kinds of people and every effort is made to involve reluctant parents.

(xvii) Parents are fully aware of the channels of communication with the governors which are open to them through the parent governor.

Appendix B3

Examples of Assessment and Reporting Information Provided for Parents

School 1

Extract from Parents' Handbook

The academic progress of your son or daughter will be monitored throughout the school and reports will be issued by the Faculties on an individual basis when appropriate; this will be at least twice a year but the particular time may vary.

Where grades are given for coursework and effort they will be based on the following scale:

Attainment in Coursework and Examinations		Effort
Outstanding	A	Outstanding
Above Average	B	Very Good
Average	C	Average
Below Average	D	Below Average
Well Below Average	E	Unsatisfactory

Parents' evenings for individual interviews with subject teachers are held regularly after the issue of reports so that you can talk personally with the staff who teach your son or daughter.

Nevertheless, if you have any queries about the academic progress of your son or daughter at any time during the year you are welcome to make an appointment with the Head of Faculty concerned, or if the query is a general one with the Head of School — Lower, Middle or Upper. Equally, a Head of School or Faculty may write to you where he feels it would be valuable, to suggest a meeting.

School 2

Extract from a covering letter sent with the report; the letter concludes with an acknowledgement return

There are two grades in each subject. Both are important:

1. *The Academic Achievement Grade* (A to E) is the letter in the first space. It denotes the boy's achievement in the subject.

   (a) *In Forms 1—3* the Academic Grade shows the boy's achievement in each subject compared with that of the other boys in his year group in the school. In each year group, grades will be awarded as follows in subjects which are taken by all boys:

   A — to approximately the top 10%

   B — to approximately the next 20%

   C — to approximately the next 40%

   D — to approximately the next 20%

   E — to approximately the remaining 10%

   In all subjects not taken by all pupils (e.g. German) grades have roughly the same value as in other subjects.

   (b) *In Forms 4 and 5* an attempt is made to equate the grade with possible future performance in Public Examinations. GCE Ordinary Level grades are expressed on an A—E scale, of which Grade A is the highest . . .

   (Performances below the standard of Grade E are ungraded.)

   A Grade 1 in CSE is equivalent to at least Grade C in GCE.

2. *The Effort Grade* (1-5) is the number in the second space. It will tell you whether the achievement grade is a true reflection of your son's capabilities. Thus a Grade 1 shows that in attitude, interest and effort, he is making the very best use of his ability. Grade 3 means that he is making only a moderate effort and therefore not doing himself full justice. Grade 5 would show that he is making little or no effort.

School 3

Extract from professionally printed and illustrated prospectus, which also includes details of senior staff, a description of the school and its method or organization and information dealing with daily routine, extra-curricular activities and the Parents' Association

REPORTS

All parents are sent regular reports on their children's progress. A progress card summarising effort and attainment in each subject is issued at the end of the Autumn and Spring terms, and a more detailed report is issued at the end of the school year. Each half term the school makes an internal assessment of pupils' progress, and parents are consulted whenever the need arises.

VISITING THE SCHOOL

It is very important that parents and teachers work together. Every year all parents are invited to attend parent/teacher evenings, when they can discuss their children's progress with their various subject teachers. Parents are also urged to make personal contact with House staff — House Heads, Assistants and Tutors — who welcome visits from individual parents, and not only when crises occur. All that is necessary is to make an appointment by telephone if possible, to arrange a time when staff needed are available.

CONTACT MAGAZINE

Two or three times a year a newsletter and magazine containing news, information and other items of interest is sent free to all parents.

Appendix B4

Example of a Survey of Parents Conducted by one of the Sample Schools

During the Spring Term parents were invited to complete a questionnaire on the Middle School Report Form. They were asked to indicate how important various types of information were as far as they were concerned and to add any comments of their own.

These are the results:

A. 417 completed questionnaires were returned to school.

B. Type of information and its importance:

Type of information	Very important	Quite important	Un-important	Irrelevant
(a) Pupil's achievement in each subject	320	64	2	1
(b) Pupil's achievement expressed as a grade	161	175	48	13
(c) Pupil's achievement expressed in writing	279	114	11	1
(d) Pupil's effort in each subject	327	83	5	0
(e) Pupil's ability to apply knowledge	252	121	14	2
(f) Pupil's external examination potential ('O' level/CSE)	250	116	18	11

Table continued

Type of information	Very important	Quite important	Un-important	Irrelevant
(g) Pupil's homework performance	136	220	38	17
(h) Subject teacher's practical advice to pupils	235	136	24	7
(i) An indication that a teacher is anxious to see the parents at the Parents' Evening	216	149	26	17
(j) Examination results expressed as a percentage	153	164	56	17
(k) Average mark/grade for the work group	110	175	80	27
(l) Pupil's position in work group	100	160	103	43
(m) Pupil's interests and achievements outside the classroom	98	195	66	42
(n) Pupil's school attendance record	142	151	55	55
(o) Pupil's punctuality record	118	169	64	50
(p) Pupil's relationship with adults and peers	161	189	21	23
(q) Pupil's character traits (honesty, industry, perseverance, etc.)	250	99	23	28

C. To the question 'Would you like an opportunity to reply to the Report?' 209 replied 'yes' and 142 replied 'no'. A number of parents felt that good opportunities to reply exist already.

D. The replies stressed two points above all others:
   1. The need to simplify our Report Forms. They obviously confuse a considerable number of parents.

2. The importance of good school/home contacts generally.

Under (1) the difficulties of interpreting grades and the preference for written comments were underlined time and time again.

A number of parents would like to see us move to a separate slips and booklet system which would provide subject teachers with much more space for written comments and, to some extent, counter the worry over a possible 'halo' effect.

It is fairly widely felt that parents are not informed clearly enough of the academic standing of the various groups.

Under (2) parents considered that whilst all headings on the questionnaire were important some information should be communicated in other ways. This included comments on effort, external examination potential, relationships, character, worries over attendance and punctuality. It was pointed out that mistaken judgements in these areas could do a great deal of harm.

E. Other points expressed
   1. We should not convey estimates of relationships, interest and character as parents are better placed to judge these qualities than we are.
   2. Reports should be positive and encouraging as far as possible.
   3. Academic comparisons are too narrow. They should relate to the *full* spectrum of ability.
   4. We are too concerned with academic results and should aim at 'better balanced' reports.
   5. A few parents felt that our present report form was satisfactory.
   6. Several wanted to receive termly Reports.

(Source: An 11—18 mixed comprehensive in the home counties)

Appendix B5

The Swindon Record of Personal Achievement: A Description

Materials used in the scheme

These consist of the following items:

The record book or file, in which a pupil compiles his record, is a four-post file of the type associated with long-term storage and retrieval, and readily withstands normal classroom use without signs of deterioration. These files are normally retained in the school until, on leaving school, a pupil is presented with his 'Record of personal achievement'.

The loose-leaf cards upon which the records are made are of good quality white card, each measuring 257 mm x 173 mm, and are supplied ready punched. The format varies slightly according to the particular events it is designed to record. Some allow for as many as 16 separate entries, while others may accommodate only a single entry, but all bear a printed title and make provision for one or more signatures. There are 28 cards including a presentation card. The latter offers a further opportunity for the head teacher and chairman of a governing body to add support to a record by their signatures upon commencement and completion. The remaining 27 cards are listed alphabetically below:

Activity	Following instructions
Art and craft	Group project work
Assignments	Hobby
Attendance	Illustrations
Away from home	Jobs
Course	Oral work
Expeditions	Personal experience
Films	Personal project work

Physical achievements	Talking with people
Radio and TV programmes	Timekeeping
Reading	Visits
Service to others	Work experience
Speakers	Writing
Sports	

Card carriers. It is a requirement of the scheme that an adult, who knows the facts of a recorded item to be true, signs the record. This necessitates transporting cards for signature, and to this end a card carrier was designed. It is basically a large plastic envelope with transparent front and strengthened back. It, too, bears the gold lettering. For internal use, manila envelopes often suffice, but the plastic card carriers have proved more than adequate to withstand the rigorous treatment associated with obtaining out-of-school signatures.

Index cards. There are eight blue divider cards, each slightly larger than the standard record card. They bear the following titles on projecting tabs and are designed to assist the placement and location of particular types of record:

Timekeeping	School courses
Work experience	Skills
General experience	Interests
Helping others	Physical fitness

The diary. Each pupil has a dairy in which to note items he may wish to record. This is of a loose-leaf, six-prong type, and spare inserts are readily available. Initially this was printed in diary form, allocating one page per day. The obvious disadvantages of wasted pages and the necessity for annual reprinting have been overcome by providing simple lined insert pages, though retaining the work 'Diary' on the front cover.

The pupil's handbook. A handbook for each pupil is also available. This is a two-ring binder which, together with printed inserts, was used to give pupils assistance in making a record by means of illustrations and text. It is now more commonly used to hold any information or work that the pupil may wish to retain.

The basic requirements are the record book and cards. Where economies have to be made, alternatives may be used for the diary, handbook, etc.

Extract from rationale provided by D. Stansbury, one-time Director, Schools Council Swindon Profiling Project

The documentation of school leavers needs to be improved because the present system gives inadequate information about personal qualities, interests, values and attitudes. It is also having an unbalancing effect on the curriculum and directing too many pupils towards clerical occupations. A bias against manual and mechanical work has been fostered in the schools by the present system of documentation. It is also necessary to provide more detailed and more reliable information about school leavers because the character and attitudes of employers is now more important to the success of business enterprises.

A personally compiled record will show the attitudes, values and priorities of the recorder because he or she has selected the items it contains and has been free to include or exclude anything. Because it is a selective record it will not contain everything a reader may want to know and must therefore be read in conjunction with other documents. It will convey information about environment, family background, lifestyles, which cannot easily be conveyed by any other document. It will also convey information about activities, interests, aptitudes, abilities and skills but this will be partial and again needs to be read in conjunction with other documents.

I have no doubt that a well designed and well organised system will motivate pupils. I am certain that it will encourage pupils to take a more positive and constructive attitude to their lives, their learning and to the business of preparing to enter work. I am convinced that recording taps a very strong motive in the young which is the need to declare an identity and to have that identity accepted by others. For this reason it is very important that the record should be personally compiled and that it should not be processed by authority or subject to a veto. Any attempt to combine a personally compiled record with a school report or with objective assessments will snuff it out completely. The motivation comes from the fact that it is personally compiled. Given this characteristic in the system, pupils will set themselves challenges and will do worthwhile things because they are making a record. As an offshoot of this, recording can improve relationships and attitudes. It does not help some by discouraging others. All pupils like to feel that their best achievements, skills and abilities are recognised and valued by the community.

Appendix B6

An Example of Reports where Grades are Linked to Subject-Specific Dimensions and Parents Informed of Course Aims

Each slip provided performance grades indicating 'Poor', 'Satisfactory', 'Good' or 'Excellent' performance and also provided space for teacher comment. Music provided grades (A—E) for both effort and attainment.

Subject	Area for assessment	
Art	Basic Design	Clay Work
	Natural/Man-made Objects	Attitude
	Use of the Media	Behaviour
	Pictorial Composition	Effort
	Collage/Matchsticks	
Art (2D)	Visual Memory	Organisation
	Imagination	Behaviour
	Observation	Attitude
	Composition	Effort
	Pattern Sense	
Home Economics	Nutrition	Confidence
	Use of Room and Equipment	Personal Hygiene
	Hygiene	Social Behaviour
	General Practical Ability	Laundry Work
	Skills — rubbing in	Effort
	— all-in-one	
	— prep. of fruit	
	and vegetables	

Subject	Area for assessment	
Metal Work	Workshop Safety Attitude Use of Bench Tools Use of Machines Jewellery	Tin Plate/ Aluminium Mild Steel Work Design Ability Effort
Music	Basic Skills Practical	History/Listening Homework
Recreational Studies	Team Games Gymnastics Minor Games Athletics/Cross Country Dance Tennis	Cricket Trampoline Swimming Others Attitude
Technical Drawing	Drawing/Design Behaviour	Attitude Effort
Textiles	Skill Originality	Behaviour/ Attitude
Woodwork	Workshop Safety Use of Tools Attitudes	Quality of work Effort

Subjects varying from the above framework:
    Humanities: Attainment and effort grades only — much more space for comment.
    Mathematics: Four test %s, 12 SMILE matrix %s.
    Science: Attainment and effort grades, test mark and year group average.

Descriptions of the course aims in each subject were printed on reverse of slips:

Subject	Description: aims of course
Art	Introduction to basic design, e.g. line, colour, texture, shape, etc. The study of natural and man-made objects, e.g. shells, plants, flowers, cogs, machines, etc. Use of various media, e.g. pencil, paint, etc. Simple claywork techniques. Pictorial composition. Project/group work, e.g. mural etc.
Art (2D)	To introduce pupils to a methodical approach to picture making. To utilise simple design elements to make more effective results. To initiate and promote correct working attitudes.
Home Economics	To give a basic training in the general principles of Home Economics. To develop the pupil's interest in the subject, to stimulate the desire to create. To learn the basic skills in the use and handling of tools and equipment. Practice in simple cookery using recipes, and to understand metric weights and cookery terms. To realise the importance of a high standard of hygiene in the kitchen. To introduce cookery related to basic nutrition — proteins, carbohydrates, fats, vitamins and minerals (foods which provide these and the nutrients' functions). Personal hygiene. Laundrywork — in relation to care of the P.E. kit.

Subject	Description: aims of course
Humanities	*Humanities*, in our *First Year*, combines aspects of English, History, Geography and Religious Education, in such a way that the children begin to understand some of the ways in which these subjects link together and overlap, whilst practising the skills traditionally associated with them. Some English is taught separately to ensure that every aspect of this vital subject is covered.
Metalwork	Safety in the workshop. A variety of materials and surface finishes. The basic skills and techniques. Elements of design.
Music	Music in Year 1 is divided into three main areas — basic skills, practical and history of music. Homework is set when relevant. Basic Skills — reading the treble clef and note values. Practical — use of the human voice, group instrumental and vocal compositions. History/Listening — a study of the orchestra, the symphonic poem and the concert overture. The Arnold Bentley test — Measures of Musical Abilities — is taken by first year pupils in the first term.
Recreational Studies	Particular emphasis is laid on safety during the first year, especially in areas such as gymnastics and athletics. For much of the time boys and girls follow a common core made up of gymnastics, dance and athletics; girls also learn the basics of netball, tennis and rounders, while the boys learn soccer and cricket.

Subject	Description: aims of course
Technical Drawing	The course introduces the pupils to the use of drawing office equipment. To draw neatly. To appreciate the designs of simple everyday articles.
Textiles	To continue the encouragement of practical skill and confidence in the use of sewing machine and basic hand sewing. To extend the area of knowledge to the textile crafts such as weaving, dyeing, collage and picture making. To promote an awareness of the construction, colour, texture and patterns of various fabrics. To use this knowledge to produce a useful and decorative item(s) using a variety of fabrics and threads, and in an individual 'design and make' project, where an item (e.g. bag/container) is planned and made for a specific purpose, chosen by pupil.
Woodwork	An introduction to the technical side of woodwork. Design using techniques acquired during the first and second years.
Projects	These vary from group to group but usually include a simple box construction and individually designed small household articles.
Mathematics	No information given on reverse of slip.

Appendix B7

A Discussion Document Provided to Staff, Parents and Governors

Reports and reporting

As we have now used all our existing stock of report slips I feel this is an appropriate time to have a look at the whole question of reports and reporting.

There are tremendous variations in the types of reports used by different schools and in the value of information contained in them. Some reports are not worth the paper they are written on; others show a very real understanding of the pupil. Parents, not all, but the majority, value as much information as they can get on their children's progress. Teachers are only too aware of the time involved in the report procedure. My own feeling is that we are accountable for what we teach in schools and that parents have a right to a report that is meaningful and constructive. Pupils too should know how they are progressing or not progressing. Therefore, if we are engaged in a reporting exercise we should make that exercise as efficient and meaningful as possible.

Perhaps the following questions will be useful in deciding whether the formula we use now is the correct one.

1. For whom are reports useful? Parents? Pupils? Teachers? Employers? Careers Office?
2. Should they be written or verbal?
3. If written, should they be augmented by parents' evenings? If so, when? (i.e. should parents' evenings be an integral and structural part of the reporting system?)
4. How often should reports be issued?
5. If written, what form should they take? Report Books? Report Sheets? Slips?

6. What should reports include? Attendance Total? Lateness Total? Effort Grade? (A–E). Attainment Grade (What assessment to be used?) Space for parent comment? Space for pupil comment? Space for Form Teacher/Year Head/Headmaster's comment?

7. If no pupil comment, should pupils have the opportunity to discuss their reports with (a) Form Teachers? (b) Year Heads? (c) Subject Teachers? Before or after reports have been sent home? How can we provide time for this to be done?

8. Should Form Teachers' remarks be a summary of subject teachers' comments?

Appendix B8

An Example of Head Teacher Initiation of Change in the Reporting System

A document produced by a newly appointed head teacher which makes clear his own views and suggests areas on which the working party should comment

1. School Reports are an essential part of the home–school relationship. They concern all pupils, teachers and parents whether they like it or not.

2. This paper is therefore directed to all members of staff, but rather than involve everyone in full staff meetings I intend that there shall be a working party of those interested in improving our system wherever possible.

3. Our supply of reports is low and will not last another year. Thus, the time is right for a reappraisal of our report system.

4. Any reappraisal we undertake must start with the consideration of the purpose of reports, and of the need of parents, pupils and staff both pastoral and academic. (Distinction between pastoral and academic is here a convenience: it is naturally appreciated that pastoral staff teach and that subject teachers care.) My own thoughts are best grouped under five headings: (a) Timing and Frequency. (b) Format. (c) Type of assessment. (d) Written comments. (e) 'Feed Back' from parents (and from pupils?).

(a) TIMING AND FREQUENCY

A staggered timetable of reports is necessary because different years have different needs: and we must avoid the danger of certain staff disappearing under a mountain of report sheets.

Need we assume that each year there should be two reports making a total of ten in a child's career from 11 to 16?

I suggest the following pattern to serve as a basis for discussion:

1st year: As soon as possible after Autumn Half Term to let parents know how the child has adapted to the new school but with the emphasis on forward looking comment.

1st year: Near the end of the Summer Term. Full report.

2nd year: Early in the Summer Term. Full report.

3rd year: Spring Term, timed to be of maximum use to staff, parents and children just before options are chosen.

4th year: After Autumn half term to provide an assessment of pupils' reaction to their new academic challenge of fourth and fifth year courses.

4th year: After Summer Half Term. Full report.

5th year: Some time before Spring Half Term. Full report for all. Pre-examination warnings valuable at this time!

5th year: End of Summer Term. Leaving certificate as proposed in Heads of Departments Meeting, September 1976.

The actual handing over of Reports should precede parents' evenings: or they could be given to parents 'on the night'.

(b) FORMAT

Just as different years need Reports at different times, so different years have different Format requirements. To avoid confusion it is probably better to think in terms of lower and upper schools.

The single sheet report is cheap, easy to store, easily duplicated. Report Books with NCR paper (no carbon required) and tear out sheets are convenient. I should like to think we can improve on the traditional Report Sheet. Certainly in the Upper School we need a change. Whatever method we choose, design and layout must receive close attention.

My personal preference is for parents to receive and keep a booklet of slips. NCR will allow copies to be kept by the school. There would be a slip for each subject thus avoiding the anomalies of space on our present Reports. (What are the hidden implications in 2 cm for RE, 4½ for English, 2½ for Science and less than 1 for Music?) The form teacher would have a separate slip. All slips would then be stapled into an attractive outer cover on which would be printed any relevant information. Ideally, we should include provision for parental comment and pupil's self assessment.

There are, of course, objections to this as to any other scheme including expense. I believe the system to be superior to the traditional reports, and I consider communication with parents a priority.

(c) TYPES OF ASSESSMENT

At a time of imminent change the whole question of standards assumes considerable importance for everyone within and without the school. Any comment on or assessment of standards tends to be comparative. Immediately one asks, 'comparative with what?'

Marks, by themselves, mean little. I once worked with a very dear lady whose lowest mark for RE never dropped below 75: and on the same staff a mathematician felt uneasy above 32. We have all met the English teacher who awards Shakespeare 16 out of 20 and marks everyone else accordingly. On some reports I have seen marks such as 69.3%, an impressive figure which suggests an attention to minute detail few of us could emulate. To be meaningful on a report, marks must be standardized — a somewhat difficult and time consuming process, the results of which are easily misunderstood.

I think marks or percentages, along with class positions, should be kept in mark books where they belong. Grades are also likely to be misunderstood, but a five point (or three point) grade scale is probably a lot safer than a 100 point mark scale. Assessment and effort grade should appear together and be explained as fully as possible.

We should always remember that marks and grades are poor things in comparison with a clearly written professional assessment of the child's performance.

(d) WRITTEN COMMENTS

The traditional report has encouraged either brevity, 'works well' or 'could do better', or minute and barely legible writing. The report slip, in theory, will encourage, lengthy, colourful, concrete and personal comment: it will avoid the staccato command, criticism or praise all too frequently met. I should be somewhat peeved if, after a year's work, my son's report read 'Mark works well' or 'must improve'.

Consideration of the needs of parents (and we have not the right to dismiss any as not worthy of our time) will lead not only to more illuminating and penetrating comment but also to a quality of tone not possible in a mere phrase or single sentence. Let us avoid the impersonal, cold note of the pedagogue which, unintentionally, raises the barrier between them and us.

(e) FEED BACK
If we are to take seriously the idea of close relationships between home
and school we should surely allow parental comment about reports. At
my last school parents were allowed 1 cm: the response was negligible.
Then we indulged in overkill and sent an A4 sheet with every report:
the response was considerable and almost entirely positive.

Is there any overwhelming reason why pupils should not be encouraged to complete a self assessment for their report? That indeed might
provide some interesting reading.

References

ASSOCIATION OF ASSISTANT MISTRESSES (1976). *School Reports: A Discussion Paper.* London: AAM.

BALOGH, J. (1982). *Profile Reports for School Leavers.* York: Longman for Schools Council.

BASTIANI, J. (1980). *Written Communication Between Home and School.* A report by the Community Working Party, University of Nottingham, School of Education.

DEPARTMENT OF EDUCATION AND SCIENCE (1979). *Aspects of Secondary Education in England. A Survey by HM Inspectors of Schools.* London: HMSO.

GOACHER, B. J. (1983). *Recording Achievement at 16+.* York: Longman for the Schools Council.

HOME AND SCHOOL COUNCIL (1975). *School Reports and Other Information for Parents.* Billericay: Home and School Council.

JACKSON, S. (1971). 'Those Bad School Reports'. *Where*, no. 54, February.

MURPHY, R. (1979). 'Teachers' assessment and GCE results compared'. *Educational Research*, **22**, 1, November.

NATIONAL EDUCATION ASSOCIATION, RESEARCH DIVISION (1970). 'Marking and reporting pupil progress'. In NEA *Research Division Report*, **1**, September.

POSTLETHWAITE, K. and DENTON, C. (1978). *Streams for the Future?* Banbury: Pubansco.

REID, M. I., CLUNIES-ROSS, L. R., GOACHER, B. and VILE, C. (1981). *Mixed Ability Teaching: Problems and Possibilities.* Windsor: NFER-Nelson.

SCOTTISH COUNCIL FOR RESEARCH IN EDUCATION (1977). *Pupils in Profile.* London: Hodder and Stoughton.

WARNOCK REPORT (1978). *Special Educational Needs. Report of the Committee of Enquiry into the Education of Handicapped Children and Young People.* London: HMSO.

WINTER, R. (1976). 'Keeping files: aspects of bureaucracy and education'. In YOUNG, M. F. D. and WHITTY, G. (Eds) *Exploration in the Politics of School Knowledge.* Driffield: Nafferton Books.

WOODS, P. (1979). 'The professionalism of school reports'. In *The Divided School.* London: Routledge and Kegan Paul.